Manny Rubio

Scorpions

Everything about
Purchase, Care, Feeding,
and Housing

Filled with Full-color Photographs

Illustrations by
Michele Earle-Bridges

BARRON'S

2 CONTENTS

PEOPLE AND SCORPIONS

Ever since humans began keeping pets centuries ago, there has been a fascination with the unusual—the more bizarre the better. The practice grew as travel flourished and has become more popular than ever. Since the 1940s, hundreds of thousands of American homes have been awakened every morning to the melodious song of a canary, the chirping of a colorful finch, or the raucous squawking of a parakeet. What child did not have at least one goldfish during his formative years?

For decades, millions of colorful freshwater and saltwater tropical fish have been imported annually from waterways throughout the world or raised in tropical fish farms. Large, magnificent parrots, cockatoos, and other parrotlike birds became so desirable and scarce that a network of smugglers founded a lucrative trade in them.

Although dogs, cats, and tropical fish remain the pets of choice, inquisitive minds have become enchanted with the more exotic animals. Animal importers suddenly have found a demand for a completely untapped resource of previously overlooked animals. The majority of these are plentiful in the wild, easy to collect and transport, and can be sold rather inexpensively. Care must be taken that overcollecting

This Arizona Hairy Scorpion (Hadrurus arizonensis) assumes a distinctive defensive position after having been rousted for the picture.

combined with habitat destruction does not severely reduce the numbers of these new "pet" species. Although skeptical, some conservationists see captive breeding as a way of limiting the impact on wild populations.

The New "Pets"

Keeping amphibians and reptiles (affectionately known as "herps") was the first of this new trend. In the past few decades, an array of insects and spiders (mostly tarantulas) have found a solid place among pet owners. Recently, scorpions have claimed a substantial following, and as additional species become available, interest in them will grow. This bias is logical; keeping smaller exotic "pets" has been a basic tenet of European and Asian animal lovers for years. These generally less costly animals have a fraction of the maintenance requirements, can be kept rather simply on a few shelves almost anywhere, and (at the very least) are equally as interesting as any other "pet."

What Is a "Pet"?

There is some question about using the term "pet." In its truest sense a pet is "an animal kept for amusement or companionship," or "an object of the affections."[1] Realistically, invertebrates can be considered amusing, in that their habits are extremely engaging, but it would be a sizable stretch to assume that they offer companionship and we can show affection toward them. If you are interested in these traits perhaps you should look to vertebrates, most particularly "warm and cuddly," highly affectionate, responsive mammals.

The Remarkable Scorpion

If you are searching for a remarkable animal whose unusual behavior and day-to-day actions will captivate and tempt you to spend hours just observing it and the characteristics that make it an amazingly efficient predator, I suggest keeping a scorpion. In a brief time, you will understand why these small creatures have survived for millions of years without undergoing major physical changes.

You Can Contribute

As old and as common as scorpions are, when compared to other land animals, very little has been written about their natural history, and only a handful of scientists are currently studying them. Although the toxicity of some species' venom is well documented, there is practically nothing known about the life histories of hundreds of others. This is an important consideration when contemplating acquiring and maintaining obscure species. Successful captive maintenance and breeding of arachnids is in its earliest stages, and much more must be learned. This affords an exciting opportunity for conscientious, dedicated keepers to observe and document previously unrecorded information.

Although emphasis has been predominantly placed on tarantulas, the two major avocational societies (American Tarantula Society and British Tarantula Society) actively solicit and print articles from serious amateur arach-

---

[1] *American Heritage Dictionary of the English Language,* 3rd ed. New York: Houghton Mifflin Co.

nologists. The Internet also provides several active sites through which a great deal of information is exchanged among a wide range of interested scorpion keepers worldwide.

A Few Things to Consider

1. One must be cautious when making generalizations about any form of animal life because there are always exceptions.

2. Very few pet shop employees, or naturalists for that matter, are knowledgeable about keeping scorpions. Pet shops with a large selection of nicely displayed and maintained tarantulas and scorpions will likely be better sources of information than those that only have a few. Asking a few key questions will quickly uncover whether you know more than the employees do.

3. Many scorpions do not have common names, and even if they do, they may vary greatly from place to place. Also, several species may be known by the same common name in different regions. Learning the scientific name not only provides the proper label for the animal, but it is universally understood what species is being referred to. This makes communicating with other keepers less complicated.

4. Generally, darker scorpions tend to live in moist, forested areas; lighter-colored forms inhabit arid and grassland environments. There are numerous exceptions. Many of these are scorpions that have coloration that matches the substrate of their environment.

5. Because of the reversal of seasons and because scorpions are more commonly found during the summer and warmer rainy seasons, those from the southern hemisphere are available in greater numbers from November through February.

6. The taxonomy (systematic arrangement) of scorpions is in dire need of revision. Much was done at the end of the 19th century and early 20th century; and there has been a recent flourish of findings and identifications. However, arachnologists believe there are hundreds of new forms waiting to be discovered and identified.

7. Scorpion keeping is a refreshingly new area of natural history that is virtually wide open to observing, discovering, learning, and teaching.

8. Scorpions with very large, bulky "pincers" usually have less toxic venom and are less likely to sting. Prey is procured by grabbing and crushing.

9. Venom from most scorpions is not considered dangerous to humans.

10. Venom toxicity varies greatly from taxon to taxon and among different animals within a species. Other variables include the amount recently expended on prey or other predators, the number of consecutive stings to this victim, and the amount injected. The amount of venom injected is controlled by the scorpion. Care should always be taken to avoid being stung. Never underestimate the potential danger.

11. Individuals are affected differently by scorpion venom. Certain people are highly sensitive to specific venoms and will react violently, whereas others may find a sting little more than a minor inconvenience.

12. The first scorpion sting may sensitize the victim to a more severe second encounter.

13. The overall length of a scorpion is measured from the anterior margin of its prosoma ("head") to the tip of its straightened metasoma ("tail"), and includes the telson.

14. Never forget that the life and well-being of a captive animal is your responsibility.

15. Experts do not have all the answers; they have more questions.

Scorpion Natural History

Natural Habitats

Scorpions live in a variety of habitats—rainforests, woodlands, deserts, grasslands, and many places in between. Most scorpions prefer warmer tropical or subtropical climates. However, some species have invaded unusual areas, a few of which may be surprising.

✔ In various regions of the world, several species of small scorpions (less than 1⅓ inches [35 mm] in length) live within the intertidal zone. Known as littoral scorpions, they eat the myriad of tiny invertebrates that thrive within seaweed, tidal wrack, and decaying sea creatures that have washed ashore.

✔ A few taxa live at elevations higher than 14,000 feet (4,200 m). *Scorpiops rohtangensis* lives at an altitude of 14,100 feet (4,300 m) in the Himalayas of Asia, and *Orobothriurus altola* lives at 14,400 feet (4,400 m) in the Andes of South America. They too are small and spend months under rocks and in burrows covered by snow and ice. Experiments have demonstrated that many scorpions can survive temperatures below freezing.

The influence of specific microhabitats, such as soil types and hardness, kinds of rock, amount of ground litter and cover, moisture gradients, seasonal temperature extremes, and prey availability all limit the distribution of scorpions. To survive for so many millions of years, scorpions have had to adapt.

One of the massive pincers belonging to the African Red-clawed Scorpion (Pandinus cavimanus) that are used to crush prey.

The Death Stalker (Leiurus quinquestriatus) has much smaller, less powerful pincers, and relies on its potent venom to subdue prey.

The pincers of the Yellow Ground Scorpion (Vaejovis confusus) are not much larger than those of the much more potent Death Stalker.

A Yellow Ground Scorpion (Vaejovis confusus) is at home among rocks or in sand.

*Many scorpions like this small **Mesobuthus martensii** are at home in loose sandy soils with rocks and other litter to hide under and find prey.*

An adult Unstriped Scorpion
(Vaejovis carolinianus) is
small enough to fit on a dime.

✔ Sand dwellers (psammophiles) have numerous setae, which increase the surface area of their long, flattened feet for better footing in loose sand. Rock dwellers (lithophiles) are flattened and elongate with thickened, pointed setae on their feet, and exceptionally have curved ungues on their feet that facilitate moving freely on and within rocks and crevasses. Their metasomas are long and thin and are carried to the side rather than being elevated like most species. A stocky, robust body with short legs and large, powerful pedipalps and pincers characterize burrowing (fossorial) scorpions.

✔ Some scorpions (troglobites) live deep in caves. Because there is no need to see in the dark, most are blind and some lack eyes completely. They usually have extremely slender, colorless bodies, legs, and pedipalps—all adaptations for living in cracks, under rocks, and in the recesses of caves. Scorpions adapted to living toward cave entrances are known as troglophiles and do not have reduced eyes and other characteristics of troglobites.

✔ Arboreal scorpions are small, lithe, and extremely agile climbers, and are frequently encountered in buildings. Some climb high into trees, living within holes and cracks in the bark, whereas others choose the basal portions of bromeliads. Since we are at the very early stages of exploring the rainforest canopy, it is probable that many new scorpion species await discovery there.

Each of these physical differences has a drawback; some species are so habitat-specific that they have difficulty negotiating other environments. This is an important consideration when attempting to keep these animals.

Adaptations for Survival

In addition to providing support, the scorpion's hard exoskeleton provides it with a rigid, protective coat that is commonly colored to match the general habitat in which it lives. This provides the scorpion with a degree of camouflage. The scorpion's flattened shape lets it squeeze into very small, tight areas. Venom-injecting apparatus and strong pedipalps, combined with a quickness to run and react, make the scorpion a formidable, dangerous warrior and predator.

Scorpions have one of the lowest metabolic rates in the animal kingdom. They can go for long periods without feeding because they can consume a great quantity of food in a single meal and because of the energy they conserve by not moving about very much.

Desert scorpions are one of the best arthropod species at conserving water. A waxy coating on their exoskeleton makes it impermeable to water (in both directions). Water intake of most desert scorpions is acquired from their food. Feces are passed in a nearly dry state, due to a high content of nitrogen and a minimal amount of water. Breathing through ventrally located spiracles and book lungs minimizes loss through respiration. Some species have flaps that cover the spiracle entrances, and they can voluntarily close them to further minimize water loss. By seeking refuge in burrows, under rocks, and in ground litter, desert scorpions avoid the hottest times of the day and thus minimize moisture loss.

Predators and Life Span

Scorpions are a meaningful part of the food chain. Aside from interspecies cannibalism, their predators include large centipedes, spiders, ants, lizards, snakes, frogs and toads, birds, and mammals.

In the American West, scorpions form a large portion of the diets of Grasshopper Mice and burrowing Elf Owls. The sand-dwelling Shovel-nosed Snake, *Chionactis* spp., also from the desert Southwest, is not only immune to scorpion venom, but appears to feed on scorpions and centipedes almost exclusively. A few other predators are resistant to scorpion venom. In Africa and Asia, meerkats, mongooses, and baboons systematically search ground litter to find scorpions and then break off the telsons or entire metasomas to avoid being stung before eating them.

· It appears that most smaller species have a short life span, perhaps 3 or 4 years. Larger scorpions have been reported to live 20 years or more. Because little is known about the natural history of most forms, there is the possibility that some species do live longer. If properly cared for, a scorpion has its best chance of surviving to old age in captivity.

Scorpions as Pets

If you have read this far you are most likely seriously considering getting a scorpion as a "pet." I suggest you spend a bit more time thinking about it.

Do You Really Want a Scorpion?

As you read, invertebrates, including scorpions, are not pets. You can expect little or no recognition of your presence. They remain secluded throughout nearly all daylight hours. It is stressful for the animal to be uncovered and disturbed, and destructive to their carefully prepared microenvironment. Nearly all their normal activities occur at night.

Most people have a negative reaction to scorpions and respond to them with revulsion. If inducing that response is a motivating factor in keeping them, I suggest you choose some other way of "proving your machismo." Scorpions, indeed all arthropods, are viewed unfavorably by many because certain people promote these misguided reactions and dispense inaccurate information.

Being Aware of the Potential Danger

There are approximately 24 species of scorpions that have been recorded as being lethal to humans. All the known lethal scorpions belong to the family Buthidae, but (as might be expected) there are reports of potentially lethal forms in other families.

Of the many thousands of people who are stung worldwide each year, hundreds (frequently estimated as more than 2,000) die. As recently as 30 years ago, the number of annual fatalities was estimated to be in the tens of thousands. Although the most dangerously venomous scorpions inhabit the deserts of northern Africa, there must be relatively few incidents of stings because these areas produce few recorded fatalities.

Most deaths occur in the rural regions of Latin America, primarily in regions of Mexico and Brazil. The culprits are usually a few highly venomous species of *Centruroides* and *Tityus,* respectively, that are abundant, actively forage, and are nimble climbers. They thrive within buildings and houses where nighttime encounters with humans are frequent. Children under the age of 3, the elderly, and persons who are sickly or have weakened immune systems, hypertension, or are extremely allergic to their venom are the primary casualties. There appears to be no correlation between a variety of allergies (e.g., peanuts or dust) and scorpion venom. Antivenom is rarely available in rural areas which are far away from major medical facilities.

The value of antivenin treatment for scorpion stings has initiated considerable debate among toxicologists when compared with the success of antivenin used for venomous snakebites. Toxicologists universally agree, however, that primary first aid and any additional treatment deemed necessary by a qualified medical attendant is the best course of action.

The potential hazard of serious consequences is compounded because of the difficulty inexperienced pet store personnel and buyers have in distinguishing the very dangerous scorpions from the many hundreds of less-life-threatening species. In fact, truly dangerous African scorpions are commonly imported for the pet trade. A recent visit to a pet shop that had a selection of scorpions nicely displayed in individual pet cages exemplified the intrinsic danger of misinformation. Placed among the more harmless scorpions was a somewhat innocuous-looking Death Stalker, *Leiurus quinquestriatus.* When the manager was told that it has the most dangerous venom of any scorpion in the world, it was removed from display. He said that it had been purchased with a variety of other scorpions from a large commercial animal jobber, and he had been assured that they were all safe to handle. This problem arose because it is fairly common for scorpion species to be misidentified when being shipped in great numbers.

Avoiding a potentially hazardous situation is the smartest kind of prevention. Because very little is known about the venoms of many scorpions and because people react differently to being envenomated, I believe that **there is no situation where a scorpion should be picked up with a bare hand.** All scorpions should be treated as though they are dangerous and never be handled. A hands-on approach is nothing other than an accident waiting to happen.

Understanding Your Commitment

An owner has an obligation to maintain any captive animal whether it is a dog or a scorpion. The keeper must be mature enough to assume the responsibility for the animal's well-being, housing, and safety. And there is the added necessity of providing absolutely escape-proof housing.

Scorpions are highly adaptable and capable of surviving under less-than-favorable conditions. Their ability to survive with little attention is not a reason to improperly care for them. Because they spend so much time in hiding, are not effusive or responsive (unless they are hassled), cannot be handled, and have relatively few needs, there is a tendency to neglect them. Like other animals, scorpions will dehydrate and/or starve if not properly looked after. All living things have a value, and you as a keeper must be responsible for their well-being.

UNDERSTANDING SCORPIONS

To the uninitiated, a scorpion looks like a lobster. Not so! They are both invertebrates (animals without backbones) and arthropods, but that is as closely related as they get. A lobster is a crustacean, and a scorpion is an arachnid. In fact, scorpions are much more closely related to spiders than to any of the crustaceans.

A Scorpion's Place in Nature

Although there are few examples, fossil evidence indicates that the earliest scorpions (400–425 million years ago during the middle Silurian) were aquatic with gills and legs and looked very much like those species living today. Some of the first scorpions to live on land (most of the time) were very small, but at least one *(Praearcturus gigas)* was huge, approximately 3 feet (1 m) in length. Now that was one big, powerful, impressive predator!

Modern scorpions have adapted to live in a wide variety of habitats—from arid deserts to moist rainforests and from below sea level to high in the mountains. One species has been found at an elevation higher than 14,000 feet (4,200 m) in the Andes Mountains. Although small in size, scorpions are an extremely important part of the food web. It is not uncommon

The defensive position of an Arizona Hairy Scorpion (Hadrurus arizonensis) *shows it to be a formidable adversary.*

for three or four different species to live sympatrically (in the same habitat), or in very dense communities. They are carnivorous, consuming a large number of invertebrates and occasional very small vertebrates to help maintain a balance between the species.

Scorpion Taxonomy

Taxonomy is defined as the science of classifying living things. As scientists learn more about a species, it is frequently necessary to reevaluate and change its classification. Sadly, few scientists are working with scorpions, so the process of accurately classifying them is evolving very slowly.

Using a variety of physical and molecular characteristics, scientists have divided the approximately 1,500 currently recognized species and subspecies of extant scorpions into sixteen families:
✔ Bothriuridae
✔ Buthidae
✔ Chactidae
✔ Chaerilidae
✔ Diplocentridae
✔ Euscorpiidae
✔ Heteroscorpionidae
✔ Ischnuridae
✔ Iuridae
✔ Microcharmidae
✔ Pseudochactidae

- ✔ Scorpionidae
- ✔ Scorpiopidae
- ✔ Superstitionidae
- ✔ Troglotayosicidae
- ✔ Vaejovidae

Many of these are split into subfamilies, which are in turn divided into genera, species, and in some cases subspecies. There is considerable debate among zoologists as to the validity of subspecies; some believe that the current classification of many subspecies is poorly defined, subjective, and unwarranted.

Because many of the physical characteristics used to differentiate taxa are very small, a dissecting microscope is needed to see them properly. Separating genera and species necessitates accurate and careful investigation and demands great patience and skill. Because the coloration and size of specimens of the same species vary from different microhabitats, these characteristics must be cautiously used as valid distinguishing characters. No single source is available to identify scorpions to the species level. With the current growing interest in scorpions, there is no doubt that many more scorpions will be discovered and described.

Scorpion Anatomy

Most people are familiar with a scorpion's shape, and all species look very much alike. Scorpions are considered very primitive compared with most other land animals. In fact, scorpions are the most ancient arachnids found so far. They have been extremely effective in adapting, permitting them to persist on land for the estimated 325–350 million years since emerging from the water.

All scorpions gather their body heat from external sources and are incapable of producing their own. In very hot environments, they are nocturnal. Some temperate and rainforest species may be active

Tarsus (Moveable Finger)
Chela (Pincer)
Manus (Tibia)
Sternum
Prosoma
Genital Operculum
Pectines
Mesosoma
Sternite
Spiracle
Metasoma
Opisthosoma
Anal Opening

Ventral view showing major external characteristics.

Dorsal view showing major external characteristics.

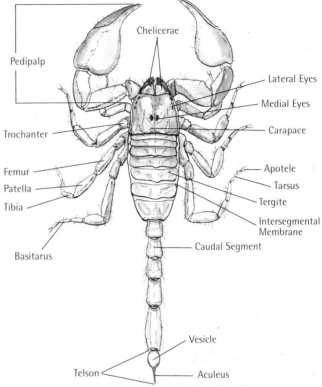

during overcast days and when the canopy prevents strong sunlight from reaching the ground.

A close look: Although it is beyond the scope of this book to discuss in detail the anatomy of scorpions, it is important to get an overview of all the body parts and their characteristics in order to identify the many different species. The most obvious external parts are discussed here, and the others can be located in the illustrations. Internally, scorpions have nervous, circulatory, respiratory, reproductive, and digestive systems.

Like all arthropods, a scorpion's body is covered by a thin, hard, exoskeleton that supports and protects the internal structures. It is the base for a variety of sensory receptors, spiracles (breathing openings), and other biologically significant openings to the outside of the body.

The Prosoma

The body is divided into two major parts: the prosoma (cephalothorax) and the opisthosoma (abdomen). Dorsally, the prosoma is covered with the carapace. The chelicerae are partially covered by the carapace and project from under its front. Chelicerae are preoral mouthparts which are used to tear and grind food; they are found in all arachnids.

A pair of median eyes and smaller lateral eyes (as many as five pairs) are located on the cara-

pace. Median eyes function as very primitive viewing organs, capable of perceiving depth and spatial relationship, as well as forming an unsharp visual image. They are very sensitive to light. Their primary purpose seems to be celestial navigation and to differentiate light and dark (e.g., day and night). Lateral eyes are as much as three times smaller than median eyes and react more quickly to working in darkness. They appear to be mainly responsive to the light–dark cycle, and to "set" scorpions' biological clocks. A light-sensitive area on the metasoma has recently been discovered in several different scorpions. Its function is not yet known.

(left) The eight button-shaped slits on the ventral mesosoma of this Blond Hairy Scorpion (Hadrurus arizonensis pallidus) are the openings that allow air to enter and leave the scorpion's body for breathing.

The Opisthosoma

The opisthosoma is composed of the wide, bulky mesosoma (preabdomen) and the elongated, tail-like metasoma (postabdomen). Seven tergites (dorsal, chitinous plates) combine to form the dorsal surface of the mesosoma. The flexible tissues that enable all the rigid parts of

(below) The telson of this wild-caught Tri-colored Burrowing Scorpion (Opisto-phthalmus ecristatus) is missing, likely from an encounter with a predator or another scorpion. It has been in captivity for more than 2 years, molted once, and is thriving. There are no signs of regenerating the important appendage.

Unlike a few of its Mexican relatives that have a potent venom, this Texas variety of the Common Striped Scorpion (Centruroides vittatus) has a painful sting, but is not considered overly dangerous.

the exoskeleton to articulate are called the intersegmental (pleural) membranes. The metasoma is made up of five articulating ringed segments and ends with a bulbous telson. The telson is not considered part of the metasoma. The needle-sharp, venom-injecting portion of the telson is the aculeus ("stinger"), and the roundish part (the vesicle) contains the venom glands. A small pointed prominence (subaculear tubercle) is located near the aculeus on some taxa. Taxonomists use this small prominence as a characteristic when distinguishing among species.

The metasoma is not a tail *per se,* but rather a continuation of the abdomen. It contains part of the intestine, the hindgut, nerves, arteries and veins, and muscles, and supports the telson.

As its name suggests the African Flat-rock Scorpion (Hadogenes troglodytes) is shaped to live in rock crevasses.

The potentially very dangerous Death Stalker (Leiurus quinquestriatus) is said to have the most potent venom of any scorpion.

The metasoma is very muscular and, aside from stinging, is used for digging, scraping dirt, balance, and climbing. The anal opening is located in the soft tissue of the last (fifth) segment, where it connects with the telson.

Appendages

Four pairs of jointed legs (all located on the cephalothorax) provide locomotion and are used for digging. The portion that connects each leg to the body is called the coxa, and is followed (in order) by the trochanter, femur, patella, tibia, basitarus (tarsomere I), tarsus (tarsomere II), and apotele. Ungues (lateral) and dactyl (median) "clawlike" appendages are attached to the apotele.

Pedipalps are analogous to human arms and hands. The pair of pedipalps has six segments. Starting at the body, they are the trochanter, femur, patella, tibia, and tarsus. The last two segments are greatly modified into "pincers" ("hands"), the manus (a modified tibia) is the palm and fixed finger, and the tarsus is the movable finger. Although most of the jointed segments are comparably named to those found on legs, pedipalps are not legs. Pedipalps are used for grabbing, holding, and crushing prey; for protection as weapons and shields; and for digging. They also carry some exceptional sensing organs.

The inside surfaces of the pincers have a series of granules and pointed "teeth" that enable them to hold tightly and crush prey. Some males have conspicuous, strongly serrated teeth that are lacking in females, making them sexually dimorphic characters. Scorpions with larger, sometimes massive pincers are capable of exerting remarkable pressure, cracking and mashing all but the hardest invertebrate exoskeletons.

The Underside

Taxonomists use the shapes of the parts of the ventral region of the body between the legs (coxosternum) to differentiate among scorpion families. The two genital opercula (fused plates covering the genital aperture) are found on the midline just behind and posterior to the centrally located sternum. Eight small spiracles (openings) on the broad sternites (ventral chitinous plates of the mesosoma) carry air into the book lungs (respiratory organs). Because they can be "closed" during times of stress spiracles are efficient in minimizing moisture.

Sense Organs

Although scorpions have very poor eyesight, they have an arsenal of highly responsive sensing receptors that would make any hunter proud. Using scent, air movement, and vibrations, they sense the presence of predators, prey, mates, water, temperature, and light, as well as several other stimuli.

Pectines

The pectines are a pair of unusual comblike appendages located on the ventral surface just behind the last pair of legs. Unique to scorpions, these organs sense ground vibrations and are used by males for sensing pheromones during mating.

Setae

Setae are hairlike projections found on many parts of the body, legs, and pedipalps, giving the scorpion a pronounced "hairy" appearance. Some are not visible without magnification. At least three different kinds of movable and immovable setae have been described. Setae receive tactile, thermal, chemical, and humidity sensations.

The most important setae are the long, thin trichobothria found only on the pedipalps. They are incredibly sensitive to air movement and airborne vibrations and can sense the slightest movements of prey, other scorpions, or threatening situations. Future research may show that some contacting the gound may pick up those vibrations as well. Trichobothria locations, numbers, and arrangement are consistent within a species and are used as taxonomic characteristics.

Tarsal ("foot") setae pick up substrate vibrations and may also sense chemicals and water and humidity. Bristlecombs (clumps of setae) on tarsal and basitarsal segments increase the surface area of the "foot" (like snowshoes), and are adaptions for expediting travel on sand. Although bristlecombs and tarsal setae are excellent clues to the habitat preference of a particular scorpion, they are not necessarily easy to notice.

Other Receptors

Other nearly microscopic receptors called slit sensilla are found on the legs and metasoma. When any pressure is placed on the exoskeleton these slits open slightly. Depending on the amount of pressure, the scorpion makes adjustments in body movements and posture. Additional slit sensilla on the basitarsae of all eight legs seem to sense ground vibrations, like those produced by the movements of insects. The scorpion uses the sensations received by the two opposing legs to triangulate on the prey and to determine its direction and distance.

Stridulation

As many as 150 species of scorpions can make sounds by stridulation—the rubbing of one part of their body against another. Some *Opistophthalmus* scorpions rub their chelicerae and cephalothorax together to produce a hissing sound. Other genera stridulate by rubbing telsons to metasomas, pectines to sternites, and pedipalps to first walking legs. *Scorpio maurus* bang their telsons on the ground, producing clicking noises. These sounds appear to be warnings to potential predators.

Venom and Envenomation

Venom is a mixture of complex chemicals (low molecular weight peptides) that destroy cellular components when they enter cells. More than 100 of these peptides have been identified in scorpion venom.

The primary function of venom is to capture and subdue prey; protection likely evolved secondarily. All but a very few extremely uncommon scorpions produce venom. Fortunately, only about 24 species are considered potentially lethal to humans. Biochemists are performing a great deal of research on venom, particularly on how it affects the human body.

Venom toxicity varies from genus to genus, species to species, and (frequently) within a species. It also tends to be somewhat specific to scorpions inhabiting a particular area. Why? Mainly because the quantity of each venom component varies. Aside from genetic inheritance, environmental conditions, the kind of prey that is most frequently encountered and eaten, or simply a normal physiologic variation between specimens may cause the differences.

The Sting

The process used by a scorpion for envenomation is quick and efficient. The muscular

The setae and needle-sharp aculeus can be clearly seen on the telson of an Arizona Hairy Scorpion (**Hadrurus arizonensis**).

metasoma is held high, telson poised, ready to deliver a rapid downward thrust enabling the needlelike "sting" to pierce the exoskeleton or skin of its target. The scorpion must be able to feel that a sting has been effective, because if the "sting" has not penetrated, the scorpion will continue to probe until it reaches its mark. Setae close to the "sting" are likely important sensors. Struggling prey may be stung several times while being held in the pincers.

The amount of venom injected can be controlled by the scorpion; greater doses for larger prey animals and less for smaller prey. In some cases, no venom is injected; this is known as a "dry sting." A similar phenomenon is seen in venomous snakes. The sting may remain imbedded for a few seconds, or simply stabbed in, then immediately removed, and returned to a ready position. No matter which method is employed, the scorpion's venom apparatus makes it an extremely efficient predator, capable of capturing larger more dangerous prey.

The reaction of humans to the stings of nearly all scorpions is minimal and most commonly equated to being stung by a bee or wasp. But others cause much more severe reactions. Of course, a few can be fatal. The pain and other reactions associated with scorpion envenomations can be of consequence—a sting is always a threat.

A ground angle view of the most dangerous scorpion in Africa, The Tunisian Fat-tailed Scorpion (**Androctonus australis**). *It has been disturbed and is in its defensive position ready to strike at the intruder.*

During the winter months,
African Flat-rock
Scorpions like this
Hadogenes troglodytes
are sometimes
available.

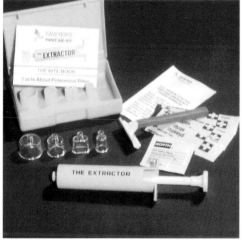

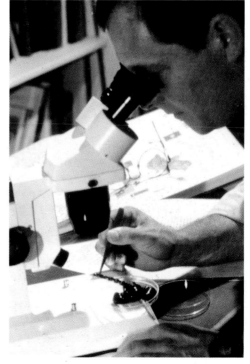

(above) The Extractor has been effective in
removing venom from venomous snakes and
stinging insects.

(right) Scientists use dissecting microscopes
to carefully examine characteristics that
differentiate species.

One factor that is normally overlooked in a sting is the possibility of developing an infection or tetanus. Tetanus is a potentially fatal disease, with more than 50,000 people dying from it each year worldwide. Some people have allergic reactions to tetanus antiserum. The most recent immunization for tetanus, an injection of *tetanus toxoid,* is considered permanent. If you are uncertain of the immunization method, a tetanus booster should be administered every few years. All scorpion stings should be treated like any small stab wound, and care should be taken to clean the wound and apply an antiseptic.

The great fear—a serious reaction: Small children, the elderly, and people with impaired or weakened immune systems, serious preexisting medical conditions, or hypertension are candidates for serious complications from a sting. The average, healthy adult usually incurs minimal reactions to a sting from all but the most toxic scorpions.

Usually, the body's defensive system will react to a scorpion sting by producing antibodies that combat the toxic components—the first time! That is the good news. The bad news is that any additional sting by a scorpion with identical or very similar toxins may sensitize a few people (make them acutely allergic). It may take several stings. You cannot tell until you are stung again. Sensitized people will have an anaphylactic reaction to subsequent stings, possibly violent and life threatening. In a worst-case scenario, the victim stops breathing, suffers heart failure, and dies—all in a few minutes. And no, this is not being overly melodramatic.

Statistics show that more people die from anaphylactic shock resulting from arthropod bites and stings than from the toxic effects of the venom. This is also true with scorpions. If you are highly allergic to some medicines, and to bee, wasp, or ant stings, you may be highly susceptible to developing a scorpion venom allergy as well.

Antivenom

Scorpion antivenom (antiserum that combats the effect of venom) is produced at a few laboratories throughout the world. Like polyvalent antivenom produced for pit vipers, a few types of scorpion antivenom seem to work on several different types of scorpion venom from closely related species. In some cases, it is more effective to use specific antivenom. For instance, *Androctonus* antivenom does not work on New World *Tityus* venom. A variety of antivenoms are produced, mainly for the more dangerous scorpions found in a particular region. Considerable debate exists regarding the efficacy of using it because so few scorpion stings are actually life threatening and because antivenom has the potential to produce a serious allergic reaction. In most cases, the antivenom is more dangerous than the venom it is treating. Most antivenom is produced by injecting horses with small doses of venom and extracting the immune bodies produced in their blood. It is the reaction to the horse serum that can cause anaphylaxis.

Experiments are being made to produce scorpion antivenom by using goats rather than horses. The venom lab at Arizona State University has produced scorpion antivenom from goats for many years, and it seems to be safe and effective.

Better Safe Than Sorry!

The preventative measures and those taken while getting to a hospital after a scorpion sting can save your life.

If you think that you are likely sensitized to scorpion venom, be prepared. An allergist can prescribe a specially designed kit *(EpiPen)* to counteract the early stages of anaphylactic shock. An *EpiPen* is a small, personal, easy-to-carry, auto-injecting apparatus for administering 0.3 mg of epinephrine. Epinephrine is a drug that induces the body to secrete adrenaline, which combats extreme allergic reactions. It is highly effective against ant, bee, wasp, and scorpion stings.

However, considerable less efficient, over-the-counter antihistamine medicines such as *Benadryl, Ephedrine, Tagamet,* or *Zantac* are worth using if an *EpiPen* is not available.

A Desensitizing Treatment

A person sensitized to scorpion venom can undergo a long-term (24-month) desensitizing regimen similar to one that has been effectively used by people who are allergic to bee and wasp stings. This regimen includes weekly injections of increasingly larger amounts of venom, followed by monthly maintenance doses. Obviously, this procedure should be reserved only for those who must work with scorpions on a daily basis. On rare occasions, or if you are really lucky, continued stings will stimulate your body to develop stronger-than-normal immunities to the toxins.

The Extractor

If used immediately, *The Extractor* is effective in removing venom of a variety of venomous snakes, stinging insects, and arachnids.

This well-designed, carefully manufactured device sucks venom out through the wound at the site of the bite or sting. However, it must be applied almost immediately (before the body has transported the venom away from the envenomation site).

Dozens of similarly designed pumps have been used for nearly 100 years with mixed results. All have had inadequacies, usually because of the amount of suction they produce. It was also thought that there was a need for cutting the wound to compensate for the inadequate suction.

No wound cutting is required with *The Extractor;* simply push in the plunger and it starts to draw. It comes with several different-sized orifices to better accommodate and localize the site of the wound. *The Extractor* produces an amazing amount of consistent, negative pressure that efficiently extracts venom. Because it can be applied very rapidly, it is much more effective than similar devices.

Some arachnid keepers question its value, mainly because of the skepticism remaining from previous designs and the somewhat cavalier approach to being stung. However, this is the only device recommended by experienced medical personnel and toxicologists as immediate first aid for venomous snakebites and scorpion stings.

Although most scorpion stings do not require medical attention, *The Extractor* may alleviate some of the pain and reaction of a scorpion sting. The kit is inexpensive and available at most sporting and outdoor stores.

COMMONLY AVAILABLE SCORPIONS

As many as 100,000 scorpions, belonging to a variety of taxa, are imported into the United States each year. Unfortunately, many die in transit, with as little as 25% surviving their first year in captivity. Poor husbandry is usually the cause of this high mortality.

At the Pet Shop

Once you have decided to purchase a scorpion, some preparations should be made for housing and feeding **before** bringing it home. The cage can be purchased at the same time as the scorpion. Selected species are discussed in depth later.

What to Look For

The primary consideration when looking for the "right" scorpion is its health. An excellent clue to its health is the conditions that it has been kept in.

✔ Is the cage substrate dirty?

✔ Are dead cricket or mealworm carcasses lying about? Mold and mites quickly contaminate a filthy cage, making it a totally unsuitable environment. A healthy scorpion will eat what it kills.

Big showy scorpions like the Thailand Forest Scorpion (**Heterometrus spinifer**) *are hardy, attractive "pets."*

✔ Is a dish with clean water available?

✔ Has a hiding place been provided to allow it to get out of constant bright light and away from annoyances?

✔ Is it in a warm place? Most of the larger species that are imported prefer temperatures of 85°F (30°C) or higher and may be lethargic and refuse food if kept too cool.

Check the animal's physical condition.

✔ Is it alert and quick to run away or assume a defensive position when touched? This responsiveness is expected and normal. A pencil is a safe tool to use for this.

✔ Does it appear emaciated or overly thin? If so, ask that it be fed a cricket or mealworm. Likely, if it is simply underfed and not too cool or overly stressed it will feed immediately.

✔ Does it have all of its appendages? Unlike tarantulas, scorpions rarely regrow more than a small part of a severed leg.

If you are not satisfied with your evaluation or if you have second thoughts, look for a different scorpion. A novice is not knowledgeable enough to save a sick or dying scorpion, and (realistically) there are very few things that can be done if it is sick.

The Best "Pets"

A novice's first scorpion should be easy to acquire, inexpensive, simple to maintain, large, long-lived, calm, slow to sting, and have mild venom. An Emperor Scorpion, *Pandinus imperator,* is the best first choice. This species is quite tolerant and will allow the keeper to quickly observe many scorpion characteristics while learning the basics needed to provide it with an adequate environment, all with practically no potential of a dangerous envenomation.

The Forest Scorpion (*Heterometrus* spp.) is another widely available and easily kept scorpion that is physically very similar to the Emperor Scorpion. However, they have a different disposition, are quicker to defend themselves, and their venom is a bit more toxic than that of the Emperor Scorpion. Two species of Forest Scorpions (*H. spinifer* and *H. longimanus*) are so similar that they are frequently sold as the same animal. All three species will use their large, powerful pincers to give a substantial pinch that can draw blood. *Pandinus* and *Heterometrus* live in hot, humid regions in moist ground litter and require some moisture to prevent their desiccation and death. One or more of these species are available year round.

You should first become knowledgeable and successful at keeping these larger types of scorpions before you assume the responsibility of other more delicate and smaller species. Inevitably, different species will be imported as the interest in keeping scorpions as a hobby increases.

Scorpions for the Novice

The following recommended scorpions are weakly to mildly venomous, terrestrial, and not prone to climb. This makes them easier to cage and less likely to escape.

Emperor Scorpion
(Pandinus imperator)

Of all the scorpions, the Emperor Scorpion (*P. imperator*) is the best scorpion for the novice. It is large, shiny, black, with bumpy pincers. This species has been the standby of the pet trade for many years. Hundreds of thousands (possibly millions) have been sold, and with recent increased interest in scorpions as pets, the annual number is constantly increasing. To limit overcollecting, a few countries have listed some species with the Convention on the International Trade of Endangered Species (C.I.T.E.S.). This listing is designed to report the number of specimens that are exported from a specific country. Permits are required for businesses and persons to import C.I.T.E.S.-listed animals.

Natural habitat: Emperor Scorpions are native to tropical Africa (Ghana, Togo, and other countries near to the Equator), where they live near the surface in tunnels in moist leaf litter and along stream banks, and under moisture-retaining ground litter. They are frequently found in great numbers near human habitation. When prey is readily available, dozens can live in dense colonies, sharing an area of a few square yards, sometimes cohabiting in the same hole. This trait permits keeping several together in a communal cage.

Description: The Emperor Scorpion can reach an overall length of more than 8 inches (20 cm). It is erroneously claimed to be the largest living scorpion in the world. However, some species of Forest Scorpions are its equal. Pregnant female Emperor Scorpions can be massive, weighing more than 1 ounce (32 grams). Male Flat-rock Scorpions, *Hadogenes* spp., attain greater lengths, but they are considerably less robust and have amazingly long metasomas. The Guinness Book of Records claims a Forest Scorpion native to rural India, *Heterometrus swammerdami,* to be the largest scorpion in the world (9 inches [23 cm]). If this record is valid, it must be a unique and very, very impressive and formidable specimen. In contrast, the cave-dwelling *Typhlochatas mitchellii* (less than ²/₅ inch [9 mm]) is the tiniest.

Pandinus is a wide-ranging Central African genus that noticeably avoids arid areas. Only a few of the 24 species are available in the pet trade. Two East African species that have varying amounts of reddish-maroon pigment in the large part of their pedipalps are the Tanzanian Red-clawed Scorpion *(P. cavimanus)* and the African Red-clawed Scorpion *(P. viatorus).* Although their body structures are similar to *P. imperator,* they are slightly smaller, quicker in their movements, and noticeably more defensive. They mainly live in fairly moist environments; however, little has been reported about their natural history. Aside from feisty males, no other known *Pandinus* spp. is as docile and unwilling to sting as the Emperor Scorpion.

Aggressiveness: The mystique associated with an Emperor Scorpion is probably caused by its ominous, impressive appearance. It is one of the least likely to defend itself by stinging, and its venom is mild. Prey is grasped and crushed by its huge pincers. It is inoffensive, almost "shy," preferring to run away or shield itself with its pincers. If cornered, however, it will assume a formidable defensive position and use its pedipalps to grab at the agitator.

Captive conditions: When housed together, care must be taken that the enclosure is big enough to avoid crowding. The animals should be similar in size and adequately fed to prevent

cannibalism. Even then, without warning, one may decide to make a meal of its cage mate. For a few days after a scorpion molts, its exoskeleton is very soft. Until it hardens, the animal is vulnerable to attack from an aggressive cage mate.

Forest Scorpions
(*Heterometrus* spp.)

The genus *Heterometrus* has been divided into five subgenera, 21 species, and 31 subspecies—thus making classification a nightmare. They are extremely difficult to accurately identify and must be distinguished by anatomical characteristics that are best seen through a dissecting microscope.

Natural habitat: Forest Scorpions range from India westward throughout southern Asia and Malaysia. Two species, the East Indian Forest Scorpion *(H. longimanus),* with nine subspecies, and the Thailand Forest Scorpion *(H. spinifer),* with two subspecies, are the most commonly obtainable. In the past, large numbers of the Indian Forest Scorpion *(H. fulvipes)* were available, but exportation from that region has become sporadic.

Description: All are large, stocky, heavy, black scorpions that look very much like Emperor Scorpions and are frequently misidentified and sold as that species. The problem is compounded because *Pandinus* and *Heterometrus* are closely related. Generally, adult *Heterometrus* have slender and smoother pincers than *Pandinus.* Although most are black, some are a rich, chocolate brown, and others have a green or blue sheen when viewed in bright light.

Aggressiveness: They differ from Emperor Scorpions in their greater aggressiveness and readiness to assume a defensive posture and

*This healthy African Burrowing Scorpion (**Opistophthalmus glabifrons**) thrives in a clean, simply furnished enclosure. Here a 5-gallon (18.5 L) aquarium with a mixture of sand as a substrate provides an excellent home. Note the water dish, stick-on thermometer, cork bark hide, and label. The cover was removed for the photograph.*

protect themselves by using their pedipalps and sting. Also, they are noticeably quicker, running in rapid short spurts. Fortunately, the reaction to their venom is only slightly more discomforting than that from an Emperor Scorpion.

Captive conditions: Another similarity between *Pandinus* and *Heterometrus* is their desired living conditions, in that they both prefer a moist, tropical forest environment, and frequently live communally. Although a large cage and adequate feeding are necessary to maintain a group, this is not recommended because they

are more territorial than *Pandinus,* and cannibalism is always a distinct possibility.

Identification: Other *Pandinus* species are still more difficult to identify because many of them have Forest Scorpion traits. Identification can be simplified if the origin is known. This may not be so easy because most exporters use common names (they rarely, if ever, know scientific names), and the animals have changed hands several times since they were captured. Importers ship to jobbers, who may ship to distributors, who ship to pet shops. Also, to many

*The Emperor Scorpion (**Pandinus imperator**) is the best first scorpion for the novice keeper. It is shown on a map depicting its range in Africa.*

*The deep, rich, blue coloration of this Forest Scorpion (**Heterometrus cyanrus**) is barely definable as it wanders among the bamboo and litter of the forest floor.*

During the winter months, African Flat-rock Scorpions like this Hadogenes troglodytes *are sometimes available.*

of the parties involved, a large black scorpion is simply that—a large black scorpion! The best identifying characteristics are the shape of their pincers and the granulations on the carapace.

Scorpions for the Expert

After you have become comfortable with your scorpion and understand the commitment you have made, it may be time to think about keeping some of the more delicate and demanding species. The following are available regularly, slightly more expensive, and offer greater husbandry challenges than *Pandinus* or *Heterometrus*.

Flat-rock Scorpions
(*Hadogenes* spp.)

The common name, Flat-rock Scorpion, aptly describes a unique genus of African scorpions (*Hadogenes*). They are distinctly flat with very long, incredibly thin metasomas. This enables them to live in the narrow spaces between rocks.

Natural habitat: The majority of the 16 species (12 subspecies) of this genus lives in South Africa and are rarely exported. Two that range into Rhodesia and Mozambique (*H. granulatus* and *H. troglodytes*) find their way into the pet trade from time to time. Although some dealers offer specimens labeled as *H. bicolor*, a South African species, its identity is questionable.

Description: *Hadogenes* are large to very large, but not heavy-bodied or massive like

Pandinus or *Heterometrus*. The maximum recorded overall length of a male *H. troglodytes* is 8.3 inches (21 cm). Their large, strong elongated pedipalps and flat pincers continue the flattened design and are well adapted for grabbing prey hiding in cracks and fissures. They also use their broad, flattened pedipalp surfaces as shields to block the entrance to their retreat. At first sight, these scorpions are so flat that they appear to have been squashed.

Aggressiveness: Many Flat-rock Scorpions are slow to run, docile, and rarely sting. The toxicity of their venom ranks among the lowest of all scorpions, causing little if any reaction in humans. Although these attributes make them highly desirable to the novice keeper, they are more delicate than Emperor Scorpions and Forest Scorpions.

Captive conditions: *Hadogenes* require dry cages with a carefully arranged and secured stack of rocks or slate providing several narrow tight-fitting hiding places. Because they are territorial, they should be kept singularly. Although they rarely drink, a shallow container of fresh water should be provided. Flat-rock Scorpions are seasonally available, usually in short supply, and relatively expensive.

African Burrowing Scorpions
(*Opistophthalmus* spp.)

Natural habitat: There are 50 species of African Burrowing Scorpions *(Opistophthalmus)* ranging throughout the southern and eastern third of Africa; most reside in South Africa. These scorpions are obligate burrowers, preferring friable, but fairly hard-packed soils in which they can dig relatively long, deep tunnels.

Description: Species vary in size from 2.5 inches (6.5 cm) to 6.3 inches (16 cm), and live in a variety of habitats.

Extensive numbers of two large species, the Yellow-legged Burrowing Scorpion *(Opistophthalmus glabrifrons)* and the Tri-colored Burrowing Scorpion *(O. ecristatus)* have been imported in the past few years. Both have stocky builds and large, broad pincers, giving them a solid appearance. Also, they are more colorful than any of the previously mentioned species. Large females are impressive, attractive scorpions; unfortunately they spend most of their lives hidden underground in their burrows.

Aggressiveness: All species will sting readily if cornered or restrained. One species, *O. carinatus,* is said to have strong venom, whereas the others vary from mild to strong. Regardless of the species, their sting is intensely painful at the envenomation site for as long as 48 hours, but without any lasting aftereffects. The pain has been equated to that produced by bashing a finger with a hammer.

Giant Hairy Scorpions
(*Hadrurus* spp.)

Natural habitat: They live in rocky deserts where they dig deep burrows in dry sandy soil. Of the eight known species, the Arizona Hairy Scorpion *(H. arizonensis)* and its subspecies are the forms that are usually for sale. It is most commonly available in late summer, having been activated by the monsoon rains inundating the southwestern deserts at that time.

Another species, the Black Hairy Scorpion *(H. spadix),* shares much of the same overall range in extreme northern and western Arizona and southern Nevada, Utah, and California, but is also found farther north through Nevada into Oregon and Idaho. Its defining characteristics are a yellow metasoma and legs and dark gray body and chela tips. A central and southern California and Mexican species, the California Hairy Scorpion *(H. obscurus),* is rarely available. Additional species are found in Mexico. However, these species cannot be imported from that country without expensive, and difficult to obtain permits.

Description: Giant Hairy Scorpions *(Hadrurus)* are the largest scorpions found in North America, 3.5–4 inches (8.9–12 cm). However, they are nowhere near the impressive bulk of any of the previously mentioned Old World scorpions. The common name of this genus refers to the prominent number of setae that are found over most of their bodies, legs, pedipalps, and telsons.

Aggressiveness: This yellow-green scorpion is rather docile, rapidly running from a confrontation. However, it will readily assume a defensive position and sting if cornered and provoked. Although its venom is considered weak to mild, pain and swelling will occur at the site of the envenomation.

Captive conditions: Because all Giant Hairy Scorpions have similar natural histories, they can be maintained under similar conditions. A 3-4-inch (7.5–10-cm) layer of dry, loamy sand is an adequate substrate for burrowing (they spend a lot of time digging), and a few flat stones or pieces of bark may be used as retreats. In the wild, they have been found in burrows as deep as 6 feet (2 m). They are territorial and must be kept alone.

For some unknown reason (possibly an environmental factor relating to tunneling and moisture), captive born young rarely survive more than a month. Also, the mother frequently cannibalizes them within a few days of birth without noticeable provocation. Very few early instars survive the ordeal of molting.

The lengthy subterranean part of their lives remains a mystery, but it appears to be a very important variable in their natural history and healthy survival.

Adults are very easy to care for, and thus are the most widely kept "pet" scorpion indigenous to the United States. They are aggressive feeders, who will gorge themselves when plenty of food is provided and then not feed again for an extended period. They are prone to fasts; healthy specimens have lived for 6 months without feeding. Hairy Scorpions are long-lived, with many living for more than 15 years. It has been suggested that if adequately fed, they will likely not need water because all of their liquid requirements will be provided from their food. These characteristics are adaptations to surviving in an arid, harsh environment, where large numbers of prey animals and water are available for only very brief periods during the year. They drink readily in captivity and should be offered water periodically.

Gold Scorpion
(Scorpio maurus)

Natural habitat: Smaller than any of the previous species, the Gold Scorpion is fre-

TIP

Water

Although many scorpions appear to survive without water, as a precaution, a shallow dish of clean water should be offered to all scorpions at least once a week. Adding pea-sized gravel or a small piece of sponge in the dish will prevent drowning.

quently available and is fairly inexpensive. The single species within the genus, *Scorpio maurus,* has been separated into as many as 19 subspecies. They are native to a large region of western Africa and the Middle East as far east as Iraq and Iran. When taxonomists begin to investigate the systematics of this species, many changes will undoubtedly be made, including some subspecies becoming full species and other subspecies being eliminated.

Description: The Egyptian Gold Scorpion *(S. maurus palmatus)* is the most commonly imported subspecies. This quick moving, chunky, small to mid-sized scorpion, 2–3.5 inches (5–8.9 cm) has a shiny, straw yellow or golden yellow body and legs with dark tips on its large pedipalps. The short, roundish pincers somewhat resemble boxing gloves.

Aggressiveness: Although their venom is considered mild, it varies considerably among the subspecies. A sting is quite painful, and some produce more severe symptoms than others. Temperament also varies. Certain specimens will readily sting if confronted, but all will grab at the annoyance with their pincers. Because of

Although they spend a great deal of time in their burrows, another southern African native, the Tri-colored Burrowing Scorpion (Opistophthalmus ecristatus), is a colorful, hardy captive.

Arizona Hairy Scorpions (Hadrurus arizonensis) are the largest North American scorpions and will do well in dry, sandy enclosures.

their disposition and the pain associated with a sting, a novice should not keep Gold Scorpions.

Captive conditions: Gold Scorpions burrow in dark sandy soils in rocky areas, with hundreds of these burrows being found in a small section of ideal habitat. With proper substrate and adequate food, a group of six to eight can be successfully kept in a 10-gallon (37.8-liter) aquarium that has been set up as a terrarium. Several small flat rocks placed about the surface will enable each scorpion to build its own hiding spot. Tunnel entrances are usually built alongside a rock.

These scorpions are very strong for their size. When digging burrows they can easily move pebbles and small rocks that are sometimes larger than they are. At night, they stand outside of their retreats with extended pedipalps and open chela waiting to ambush passing insects. If this method is ineffective, they will move about in search of prey.

Many keepers claim that these scorpions do not do well in captivity, rarely living longer than a year. Because most are caught as adults, it is likely that they simply have a shortened life span. Some keepers speculate that a soil moisture gradient within the burrow may improve survival. This gradient may be the key to keeping many desert taxa.

Scorpions to Avoid

Many potentially lethal scorpions are occasionally available, but should be left only to the most experienced keepers. And even experienced keepers should be sure they want to assume such a potentially dangerous responsibility. All scorpions are amazing escape artists, and because they are nocturnal and can hide in

incredibly small spaces, they can be very difficult to find. You must consider not only the
threat to your own safety, but also to that of
others. **A novice should never attempt to
keep any of these scorpions.**

Death Stalker
(Leiurus quinquestriatus)

Natural habitat: Native to the rocky desert
regions of arid North Africa and the Middle
East, the Death Stalker spends the daylight
hours in burrows and scrapes that it has
cleared under ground litter and rocks. Abundant in some areas, it is frequently encountered at night actively searching for small
invertebrates on the ground, on stone walls,
and in bushes. Although it may occasionally
enter a house, it is most common in rural areas
where prey is prevalent. Currently, there is only
one species in the genus, and it is very wide
ranging. Three subspecies have been described.

Description: The Death Stalker could easily
be (and has been) misidentified as a harmless
species. Its medium size (3.5 inches [9 cm]) and
thin, nondescript appearance (amazingly similar
to dozens of other scorpions found throughout
drier regions of the world) give this scorpion a
somewhat innocuous appearance.

Aggressiveness: Their sleek, tan bodies, pale
greenish-yellow legs, long, thin pedipalps and
metasoma (except for the darker fifth segment) give *Leiurus quinquestriatus* a graceful
appearance. Do not be misled; they are quick
to move and quick to inject extremely potent
venom. In North Africa, Death Stalkers cause
85% of the reported stings, and 90% of the
deaths caused by scorpion stings. Sometimes
known as the Five-keeled Gold Scorpion, its
more recently fabricated common name, Death

*A mid-sized to small Gold Scorpion (**Scorpio
maurus**) is an attractive but feisty captive
that requires little space to keep properly.*

*Because they are very venomous and very
quick to sting, a novice should never keep
Death Stalkers (**Leiurus quinquestriatus**).
Advanced keepers should think long and
hard about the potential danger,
responsibility, and liability.*

Stalker, is much more fitting. Hopefully, this new name will be accepted because it instills an indelible, albeit dramatic, impression of its lethal potential. The name has been debated among the "purists" because of its melodramatic overtone, but I prefer and will use Death Stalker in the remainder of this book.

Because few victims of Death Stalker stings have the initial symptoms usually associated with most serious scorpion envenomation (pain, muscle contractions, excessive salivation, respiratory irregularity, twitching and convulsions, an unstable pulse rate, and erratic body temperature), the seriousness of a sting is often initially underestimated. If not properly cared for, the patient may go into shock, develop progressive respiratory paralysis, have pulmonary edema (fluid in the lungs), and heart inflammation. The eventual result will likely be heart failure. This scorpion is capable of killing adult humans, although most deaths have been children. *Leiurus* venom is the most toxic of any scorpion known.

Fat-tailed Scorpion
(*Androctonus* spp.)

Natural habitat: Eight species of *Androctonus* are found from northern Africa into Pakistan and western India. The most dangerously venomous species is the Tunisian Fat-tailed Scorpion, *A. australis*. It is found throughout arid northern Africa, frequently occurring in the same environment as *Leiurus*. It also lives primarily in a burrow or scrape under rocks and ground litter, but will inhabit loose sand as well. It is slow and deliberate in its movements, but capable of quick, short bursts of speed when necessary. The slightest movement of air solicits a defense reaction. It does not climb

well, but is much more frequently found in urban areas and houses than *Leiurus*, posing a serious threat to humans.

Description: Specimens range in color from all yellow-brown to yellow-brown with black pigmentation on the last metasoma segment and pincers. At one time, these color variants were described as subspecies. They are approximately the same length as the Death Stalker (2.5–4 inches [6.5–10 cm]), but are considerably stockier with noticeably thicker metasomas. This thick metasoma is the reason for their common name, Fat-tailed Scorpions.

Aggressiveness: Its venom is not as potent as that of *Leiurus;* however it injects a far greater quantity, making it a serious threat to humans. Its toxicity has been equated to cobra venom.

Two other occasionally imported species in this genus, *A. amoreuxi* and *A. bicolor,* have slightly less potent venom, but are still dangerously toxic. *Androctonus amoreuxi* is mostly yellow-brown, and prefers sandy areas and dunes, where it lives in a burrow it digs or in one dug by another animal. It moves slowly when foraging, but is extremely fast and quick if aroused.

Yellow "feet" contrasting with a dark olive-brown or black body, and long, thinner pincers make *A. bicolor* easier to identify. It is most common in areas of darker sand and soils with rocky patches, where it lives in scrapes under large flat stones and in animal burrows. It is more agile than the other *Androctonus* spp., and it stings with little provocation.

Many of the U.S. troops stationed in Saudi Arabia during Operation Desert Storm were stung by another species, *Androctonus crassi-cauda.* Because the incidents were considered minor, very few were actually reported. There were no fatalities. However, it still must be considered a potentially dangerous scorpion.

Like most scorpions, Fat-tailed Scorpions are sit-and-wait, ambush predators, ascending to the entrance of their hideouts at dusk to sit, with open pincers, awaiting an unfortunate passing small animal. All scorpions will forage if they need to.

African Thick-tailed Scorpions (*Parabuthus* spp.)

Natural habitat: African Thick-tailed Scorpions live in a variety of hot, arid, sandy, and gravelly environments throughout southern and eastern Africa. Various species have adapted to different habitats; some are obligate burrowers, whereas others are not. Females burrow more frequently and more extensively than males. Burrows may be very long but are barely a few inches below the surface and usually follow a spiral course. A few species inhabit sand dunes.

Although most Thick-tailed Scorpions live in South Africa and a few are exported, a majority from nearby countries make their way into the pet trade. The Mozambique Fat-tailed Scorpion, *P. truculentus*, formally known as *P. mossambicensis*, is sometimes available. Specimens of a complex group of very similar subspecies of *P. liosoma* are seen regularly.

Description: *Parabuthus* is the last major group of potentially dangerous, mid-sized to large scorpions (3.5–5.5 inches [9–14 cm]) that are found in the pet trade. Their characteristically thick metasomas and stocky shapes make them easy to confuse with *Androctonus*. Many, if not all of the 27 species and 27 subspecies, stridulate when aroused.

Their coloration is as variable as their choice of habitats. Some species are black and others are light tan, with a range of combinations and shades in between. Color is not a primary characteristic when defining a species. Color variations are a common phenomenon in a taxon that inhabits an area with soil or rocks of different types and hues. The scorpion is less likely to be seen because it uses its color as camouflage.

Aggressiveness: Although their venom varies in potency, deaths from at least three species, *P. transvaalicus*, *P. granulatus*, and *P. capensis*, have been reported, but they are not usually life-threatening. The last species has the most potent venom, but it has a very limited range and is not found in larger cities. It never enters the pet trade; the other two are exported infrequently. Regardless of the potency, their sting causes intense localized pain, stiff joints, general paralysis, and a variety of debilitating systemic effects.

The Black Thick-tailed Scorpion, *P. transvaalicus*, is the most unusual species. Its somber, matte black color, heavy, stocky body, and thick metasoma give it a nasty appearance. It is aggressive, quick to sting, and has powerful venom. When agitated, it assumes an imposing defensive position and stridulates by rubbing its telson on special rough textured areas on its metasoma, producing a raspy, clicking sound.

If this is not enough, it can spray its venom. When further provoked it continues to stridulate, which seems to "charge" the glands in its telson. It then elevates its metasoma and squirts a fine mist of venom, as far as 3 feet (1 m) at the annoyance.

Venom sprayed into an eye is extremely painful and can possibly cause semipermanent damage. Needless to say, any encounter with

The Tunisian Fat-tailed Scorpion (Androc-tonus australis) causes more deaths than any other African species. Needless to say, this is not a scorpion for most keepers.

Let the somber, dark coloration and prominent metasoma of the Black Thick-tailed Scorpion (Parabuthus transvaalicus) be a warning, it is very quick to inject a sizable dose of its venom.

P. transvaalicus should not be taken lightly. A few other *Parabuthus* species have the ability to spray venom as well.

Bark Scorpions
(*Centruroides* spp.)

Natural habitat: The 41 species (with 24 subspecies) of Bark Scorpions are found throughout North America, Central America, northern South America, and the West Indies. The potency of their venom varies greatly from species to species. One common species found in Arizona and New Mexico, the Arizona Bark Scorpion (*Centruroides exilicauda,* formerly *C. sculpturatus*), is considered to be the most dangerous scorpion in the United States.

Description: Bark Scorpions are mostly small (1.5–2.25 inches [3.8–5.7 cm]), but the elon-

gated slender metasomas of some males give them greater overall length of 3 inches (8 cm). They live in a variety of environments from deserts to moist forests. Scorpions from arid regions prefer a slightly moist niche within otherwise dry areas. They are found under loose bark, inside rotting cactus, in cracks and holes of trees, in bromeliads, among palm fronds, under leaves, trash, and surface litter, in rock piles—anywhere that maintains some moisture, provides shelter, and harbors prey. This includes houses—both rural and urban. Bark Scorpions are excellent climbers. In some regions, cow manure is commonly used as cover. Others may be found foraging in open sandy areas.

Bark Scorpions are fast runners and will sting at the slightest provocation. When first uncovered, they freeze. If touched, they respond immediately with a few rapid stings, then run out of sight, hiding in a crevice or other dark place. Most envenomations occur from unseen scorpions. In most instances, these scorpions are accidentally encountered when they are clinging to the underside of a rock, bark, lumber, or other objects where they are easily and accidentally grabbed.

They are very active nocturnal foragers, and because they are so mobile, they find their way into many unexpected places. Stories abound about them climbing into bedding, clothes, shoes, and other things in the human environment. Stepping on one while walking barefooted in a darkened house is a common way of being stung. Bark Scorpions have even been known to fall from the ceiling onto a sleeping person. Encounters are very common in many southwestern areas.

Aggressiveness: Some arachnologists believe that *C. exilicauda* is only slightly more of a threat than the equally common species found throughout the south central states, the Common Striped Bark Scorpion *(C. vittatus)*. Although both have caused deaths, they are not as lethal as a few other Bark Scorpion species. Although scorpion stings are common in the southwestern United States, the wide availability of doctors, hospitals, and antivenom has all but eliminated deaths, with none being recorded in the United States since 1968.

However, people of Mexico are prone to frequent encounters with scorpions because of their lifestyle. A few Mexican and other Latin American species are extremely dangerous. Thousands of deaths from Bark Scorpions used to occur annually in Mexico, mostly from *C. elegans, C. exilicauda, C. infamatus, C. noxius,*

The Mozambique Fat-tailed Scorpion **(Parabuthus mossambicensis)** *is sometimes available in the pet trade, but buyers should be wary of the potential of their venom.*

A small, fast, and quick to sting Arizona Bark Scorpion **(Centruroides exilicauda)** *may go unnoticed as it clings to the underside of a rock. Many stings occur in this way. Do not let their size fool you, their venom packs a serious wallop.*

C. suffusus, and *C. limpidus.* In the past few years, the availability of antivenom, combined with education and eradication programs, have dramatically lowered the annual mortality rate. Still, as many as 800 deaths are attributed to 100,000 stings annually.

The most unusual reported sting (actually several stings) was to a professional football player in Phoenix who was dressing for a game and partially crushed an Arizona Bark Scorpion that was hiding in his jersey. The player received antivenom (probably totally unnecessary) and played in the game without further problems.

The Slenderbrown Bark Scorpion, *Centruroides gracilis,* is frequently available in the pet trade. Most specimens are collected in Florida and have mild venom. However, like most Bark Scorpions, they are quick to defend themselves and stings are common. Unless there is an anaphylactic reaction, the symptoms (pain and a burning sensation at the site of envenomation) will dissipate in a few hours. This species prefers a slightly moist (not wet) environment and many places in which to hide. A light weekly misting is recommended. It does well communally if sufficiently fed. A tight fitting lid is a must as they climb well and are incredibly adept at escaping through the smallest cracks.

Fortunately, the venom of most species of *Centruroides* is not life threatening and causes reactions ranging from minor discomfort to prolonged severe pain. It is important to caution that very little is known about the affects of the venom of many Bark Scorpion species. To avoid problems, less-experienced keepers should not attempt to maintain the exotic *Centruroides* species that are occasionally imported from Central America.

Devil Scorpions
(*Tityus* spp.)

Although very rarely for sale in the United States, the danger some species of *Tityus* present makes them worthy of being singled out.

Natural habitat: Devil Scorpions live in almost any damp area. *Tityus* have been known to reach incalculably large numbers in older urban areas, where they thrive under houses and amid the rubble and trash associated with dilapidating neighborhoods. They climb well and will live in a variety of trees. Banana plants offer ideal habitat, and these scorpions pose a serious problem to agricultural workers.

Description: Approximately 100 species of these small to medium scorpions (1–3.75 inches [2.4–9.5 cm]), many of which closely resemble *Centruroides* in shape and coloration, are spread throughout the West Indies and Central and South America. Most are moderately venomous, but a few are responsible for high mortality. In Brazil, *T. serrulatus* and *T. bahiensis* are the most deadly, causing more than 100 deaths each year. The latter species retains that dubious honor in Argentina, while Trinidad has *T. trinitatis* as its main nemesis.

Aggressiveness: Envenomation victims suffer hypersensitivity, localized pain, high fever, and profuse sweating and salivating, difficulty in swallowing, vomiting, numbness of the limbs, muscle contractions, and convulsions. In extreme cases, there is a loss of consciousness, with the victim lapsing in and out of a coma. Symptoms may persist for as long as one week. Reactions to the more venomous Bark Scorpions are similar.

Common American Scorpions

With the exception of the northeastern and upper midwestern states, there is probably some species of scorpion living in your area. There are approximately 90 different scorpion species and subspecies in the United States. The Northern Scorpion *(Paruroctonus boreus)* makes its way into the extreme south of western Canada. Giant Hairy Scorpions are the largest, with the others being mid-sized or smaller. Although only the Arizona Bark Scorpion *(Centruroides exilicauda)* is the most potentially dangerous, the Common Striped Bark Scorpion *(C. vittatus)* has been known to have caused human deaths. These two species are very common, frequently encountered, and responsible for hundreds, perhaps thousands of stings (but no recent deaths in the United States) annually.

The Common Striped Bark Scorpion has been found in some southern cities. Most likely, they were transported from Texas, sequestered in packing materials. At least three small colonies are established in North Carolina, interestingly adjacent to barbecue restaurants. It appears they were carried in loads of mesquite wood from Texas. There is little doubt that additional colonies that have followed the same route will be discovered.

Eastern Bark Scorpions

Three other weakly to mildly venomous *Centruroides* are found in the United States—the Florida Bark Scorpion *(C. hentzi)*, the Bahamas Bark Scorpion *(C. guanensis)*, and the Slender-brown Bark Scorpion *(C. gracilis)*. The last is a dark brown, mid-sized species, ($3^1/_2$–$4^5/_8$ inch [9–11.2 cm]) that is widely distributed throughout the Caribbean and northern Latin America.

It appears to have been introduced into Florida many years ago, likely in cargo, and is fully established in many areas, mostly south of Gainesville. It is less likely to sting than the other indigenous Florida scorpions, and the results are about equal to that of a bee or wasp sting.

Because the small Bahamas Bark Scorpion (1.75–2.75 inches [4.4–7 cm]) has such a limited distribution in the United States (the three southernmost Florida counties), it quite likely was introduced from another portion of its range: Cuba, Dominican Republic and Haiti, and the Virgin Islands. The small Florida Bark Scorpion (1.5–1.75 inches [3.8–4.4 cm]) is found statewide (except in the southern Keys), and in extreme southern Georgia and Alabama. Colonies have also been located in North and South Carolina. These scorpions are little threat to healthy adults, usually causing nothing more than local pain and burning at the site of a sting that may last a few hours.

Western Scorpions

The southwestern United States is home to a wide variety of families and species. California boasts 58 forms and Arizona is second with 38. Texas has 18, three of which are currently being described, followed by New Mexico and Nevada with 14, and Utah with 11. To the Northwest, Idaho has 5, Oregon 4, and Washington 2. The other western and central states have at least one species each.

Vaejovid Scorpions
(*Vaejovis* spp.)

The complex genus *Vaejovis* contains as many as 60 species. They live in a diversity of habitats throughout the southeastern and

Two variations of the same species of the Slenderbrown Bark Scorpion (Centruroides gracilis) carry different venoms. The smaller one from Florida has mild venom, while those imported from Central America is said to have stronger venom.

southwestern states, Mexico, and as far south as northwestern Guatemala. The genus is divided into several closely related species groups and is currently being reassessed. Most likely, many changes in their classification will be made involving establishment of new species or possibly new genera. *Vaejovis* do well as captives if they have some moisture available. Unfortunately, they are short-lived, rarely surviving more than 4 years. Adults may live only 1 year. They climb readily and are frequently misidentified as the more venomous Bark Scorpions.

One species, the Southern Unstriped Scorpion *(V. carolinianus)* is the only scorpion in Virginia and Kentucky and ranges widely in the southern Appalachian region of Georgia, South Carolina, and Tennessee, and northeastern Alabama. This small to medium scorpion (2–3 inches [3.7–5.1 cm]) varies in adult size and coloration (from tan to dark brown) throughout its range. Many colonies contain only small adults. Its slender build and secretive habits make it appear less prevalent than it is. In some areas, it is abundant in rock and wood-

piles, under loose bark, in rotted logs and stumps, and almost every other similar woodland niche that provides some moisture and food. It is very fast, choosing to run and hide when uncovered. Although it will readily sting, the reaction is usually less painful than that of a bee or wasp sting.

Other American Scorpions

The names of the United States' taxa read like a tongue-twisting Latin lesson. In addition to the previously described genera—*Centruroides*, *Hadrurus*, and *Vaejovis*—there are *Anuroctonus*, *Diplocentrus*, *Paruroctonus*, *Pseudouroctonus*, *Serradigitus*, *Smeringurus*, *Superstitionia*, *Uroctonites*, and *Uroctonus*. A total of 65 species and 23 subspecies are currently recognized.

You should learn the basic techniques of keeping scorpions by acquiring one of those listed earlier before you attempt the smaller, generally more delicate species. When you are ready, much can be learned about the habits of a species by observing the habitat in which it is captured.

✔ Does it live in open sandy areas or among grasses?

✔ Was it found under a rock, on the surface, or in a burrow?

✔ Did it climb to its hiding place?

✔ Was the microhabitat dry or moist?

Collecting Scorpions

Here's one of the most fabulous attractions of collecting and keeping scorpions.

Walking through a brushy desert, using only ultraviolet (UV) light to pierce the blackness of the night is like opening a door to a mysterious, magical world. As your eyes acclimate to the eerie, magenta luminescence nearly everything becomes monochromatic, difficult to discern. Shadows produced by plants, rocks, and debris assume a soft, surreal aura. An array of flying insects that would normally go unnoticed annoyingly flock to the light. Moths become insidious, dive-bombing pests. Each white, man-made piece of litter (particularly plastic bottles) glows with a piercing brilliance, forcing you to squint to avoid its jarring radiance.

Eventually it happens—your eyes fix on to the unmistakable, luminous, blue-green form of a scorpion several feet away. You move toward it, mesmerized, enchanted by the ghostly vision. Applying a swift but gentle grab with your forceps, you lift it from the ground and hastily place it in a small, clear, plastic container. Bathed in the light of your flashlight, you examine the magnificence of your prize. For a brief time, you are absorbed; you gloat at your success. Turning off the flashlight, you reacclimate to the UV light and continue the quest. There will be many more such pleasurable incidents that night. Each capture is its own reward.

Almost impossible to see in the dark ground litter, an Emperor Scorpion (Pandinus imperator) "glows" when shined with a black light.

Black Lights

The availability of low-cost, portable UV lights (black lights) has made scorpion hunting fun and very rewarding. In the past few years, a few companies have made compact, self-contained, battery-powered UV lights for anglers. They were designed to simplify baiting hooks at night when using fluorescent monofilament line. Two versions are available: one has a built-in rechargeable battery and the other uses 6 "C" batteries. The fixture provides two different wavelengths of light, two UV fluorescent tubes are on one side, and a regular fluorescent is on the other. They are controlled independently and have built-in reflectors.

By replacing the regular tube with one of the UV tubes and using it as a single black light source, the batteries last longer. With the reduction in battery drain, UV light intensity of the single tube increases, and you have a spare bulb if it is needed. Plastic and glass absorb UV, so removing the plastic shield is helpful. An accessory soft case makes transportation simple and provides a place to keep extra batteries or the 115-volt AC charger provided with the rechargeable version.

Another portable UV light that has been used for several years is a slightly modified fluorescent camp lantern. It uses two tubes and a pair of large, rectangular, 6-volt batteries. They are available in stores that offer camping supplies. The bulbs can be ordered from a hardware store. Because the lamp has been designed to produce a 360-degree spread, a reflector made from aluminum foil should be affixed to direct the light. Although the lantern is heavier than the fishing light and a bit awkward to use, it is the type of item that is widely available and frequently found at garage sales. Be certain to buy gas-filled, fluorescent tubes that emit the proper wavelength of light (type "B"). Filament bulbs (tungsten) that are coated to produce UV will not work.

A professional UV light is sold through scientific supply houses. Its fluorescent tube is larger, and the heavy, cumbersome battery (made for a motorcycle) must be carried in a pack and attached with a wire. It is brighter, but its awkwardness, weight, and much higher price make it less desirable for all but the most ardent hunters.

A few cautions: Black lighting does have some drawbacks. Shorter wavelengths of UV light can cause eye damage if protection is not used. The units described above are long wavelength, so there is little danger. Those who wear eyeglasses, especially if they have an extra UV coating, are likely sufficiently protected. If you are concerned, consult with your doctor or an eye specialist about acquiring and using inexpensive, nonprescription, plastic goggles. Regardless, some people find that extended viewing with black light causes headaches because of the low light level, monochromatic rendering of everything, or eyestrain.

It is important that you move slowly and cautiously to avoid having a dangerous encounter with a venomous snake, a cactus, or any number of other stinging, stabbing, or tripping obstacles. Many hunters have been painfully surprised by unknowingly disturbing an ant mound. This can have very serious consequences if they are Harvester Ants, *Pogonomyrex* spp., the most toxic North American ant genus, or the imported Fire Ant, *Solenopsis wagneri*. Outdoor supply stores sell inexpensive canvass "chaps" that offer a great deal of protection from larger obstacles.

Most objects do not fluoresce; they simply blend into the monochromatic, magenta light. Wearing snake-proof boots or leggings definitely helps avoid injury from snakes and cactus. Also, you should stop periodically to get your bearings because it is very easy to get "turned around" or lost when you are searching intently.

Avoid Being Stung

There is always the possibility of being stung, and some precautionary measures should be taken. First and foremost, avoid physical contact with the scorpion. Although some arachnologists have few qualms about "tailing" scorpions (grabbing them by their telson and the last segment of the metasoma), the procedure is unnecessary, foolhardy; and possibly very dangerous.

A pair of 10-inch, rubber-tipped forceps is the best method. They are available from most pet shops that sell scorpions and via mail order from scientific supply houses and some reptile dealers. For larger species, some collectors prefer steel kitchen tongs with soft rubber padding attached. When black lighting paint the tips with fluorescent paint so that you can see exactly where they are relative to the scorpion. A variety of small bottles of this paint are available in craft stores and hobby shops. Incidentally, forceps are an excellent tool for removing cactus spines.

To Take or Not to Take

In some localities, certain species may be extremely abundant. In some plots of sandy desert, a hundred or more of *Smeringurus mesaensis* (formerly *Paruroctonus*) can be seen in a few hours. Occasionally visiting a particular spot and being mindful to take just a few scorpions will not seriously endanger a population. Research has shown that a very small percentage of the inhabitants are on the surface at any given time. However, continuous, relentless collecting (as has been done in parts of Togo and Ghana with *P. imperator*) can and will eventually eliminate the densest colony.

A collector must never take more scorpions than can be properly and adequately cared for. Be extremely careful to replace rocks, logs, bark, or any objects that are moved or turned to prevent irreparable habitat destruction. This is imperative where ground cover is minimal and moisture is at a premium.

Tables of Captive Conditions

The scorpions listed in these tables are the taxa most frequently available in the pet trade. Not all are addressed in the text, but the information in these tables should enable proper care.

TIP

What to Carry in the Field

Always carry a flashlight with fresh batteries as a normal light source, and a small pocket light as a smart backup. Have a partner as a safety factor, and enjoy sharing the experience. A small backpack or a vest designed for fisherman or photographers (with pockets everywhere) makes carrying containers, spare forceps, a bottle of water, a flashlight, extra batteries, a compass, *The Extractor* and/or *EpiPen,* and other things you might want, effortless.

The table **Potentially Life-threatening Species** is comprised of those taxa generally considered to be extremely dangerous. They have been included so that their husbandry data are available to persons that may require them. I emphatically suggest that they should not be maintained by anyone other than very experienced keepers and then only with full knowledge of the danger and possible implications they carry.

Eventually, arachnologists may find that some of the species included here are a complex of species that will be reassigned or described as new species. Also, be aware that many scorpions look very much alike, and dealers frequently misidentify them.

The species are presented alphabetically for simplicity.

The taxa listed in **Potentially Life-threatening Species** are considered to be harmless or moderately venomous. Their venom most likely will not cause death in adult humans. A few are excellent scorpions for the novice keeper. Remember: All scorpion stings (envenomations) cause reactions. Some people have much more severe reactions and complications than others. The best preventative is not to be stung.

The taxa listed in **Relatively Harmless Species** are considered to be potentially dangerous or very dangerous and capable of causing human deaths from the toxicity of their venom. Also, the toxicity may vary among specimens of the same species. Considerable thought should be taken before deciding to keep any of them. **Novice keepers should not, under any circumstances, attempt to keep any of these scorpions.**

Potentially Life-threatening Species

	Family	Danger	Habitat	Substrate	Burrower	Climber
Androctonus australis	Buthidae	(5)	A	CR	Y	N
Androctonus bicolor	Buthidae	(4)	A	CR	Y	N
Androctonus crassicauda	Buthidae	(4)	A	CR	Y	N
Buthus occitanus (2)*	Buthidae	(4)	A	CR	Y	N
Centruroides exilicauda	Buthidae	(3)	G	CRB	M	Y
Centruroides gracilis (4)*	Buthidae	(4)	GFT	SPB	N	Y
Centruroides limbatus	Buthidae	(3)	GFT	SB	M	Y
Hottentotta trilineatus	Buthidae	(3)	AG	CR	M	N
Leiurus quinquestriatus	Buthidae	(5)	A	CR	Y	O
Mesobuthus martensii	Buthidae	(3)	A	CR	Y	N
Parabuthus liosoma	Buthidae	(3)	AG	CRB	Y	O
Parabuthus transvaalicus	Buthidae	(3)	AG	CRB	Y	N
Parabuthus mossambicensis	Buthidae	(3)	AG	CRB	Y	N

(1) *Buthus occitanus* is the darker colored European morph with a moderate venom.

(2) *Buthus occitanus* is the yellow-colored North African morph with a more toxic venom.

(3) *Centruroides gracilis* Florida have moderate venom.

(4) *Centruroides gracilis* Central American and Cuban examples are claimed to be nearly as toxic as *Androctonus australis.*

Legend (for both tables):

☠ = very mild venom	B = bark	⇓ = low
☠☠ = mild venom	C = composite sand or	⇑ = high
☠☠☠ = moderate venom	tamped	⇒ = moderate (humidity)
☠☠☠☠ = dangerous	P = peat and mulch	± = more or less
☠☠☠☠☠ = very dangerous	R = rock	– = to, between
	S = soil (potting mix)	? = not sure or may vary
A = arid		
D = damp (not wet)	H = heavy	1×2 = once or twice a week
G = grassland/savanna/	L = lightly or light	4± = monthly (more or less)
temperate	M = moderately or moderate	W = weekly
F = forest	N = no or never	~ = Winter cool period
T = tropical	O = occasionally	suggested (10–15°F
	Q = quick	lower)
	V = very	
	Y = yes	

Communal	Aggressive	Speed	Optimal Temp F°	Optimal Temp C°	Humidity	Mist	When	Water Dish
N	V	Q	85±	29.4±	V⇓	VVL	4±	O
N	V	Q	85±	29.4±	V⇓	VVL	4±	O
N	V	Q	85±	29.4±	V⇓	VVL	4±	O
N	N	Q	85±	29.4±	V⇓	VL	N	Y
Y	M	Q	80±	26.7±	⇓-M	VL	O	Y
Y	M	Q	75+	23.9+	M	M	W	Y
Y	M	Q	80±	26.7±	M	L	O	Y
N	M	Q	80±	26.7±	⇓-M	VL	O	O
N	V	Q	85+	29.4±	V⇓	VVL	4±	O
Y	M	Q	80±	26.7±	⇓	VL	O	O
N	M	M	80±	26.7±	⇓-M	L	O	Y
N	V	M	85±	29.4±	⇓-M	VL	O	Y
N	M	M	80±	26.7±	⇓-M	VL	O	Y

Relatively Harmless Species

	Family	Danger	Habitat	Substrate	Burrower	Climber
Babycurus jacksoni	Buthidae	🦂🦂?	G	CSB	Y	O
Bothriurus bonariensis	Bothriuridae	🦂	G	S-PB	Y	O
Brachistosternus ehrenbergi	Bothriuridae	🦂🦂	AG	CR	M	N
Buthus occitanus (1)*	Buthidae	🦂🦂	AG	CRB	Y	O
Centruroides gracilis (3)*	Buthidae	🦂🦂	GFT	SPB	N	Y
Centruroides hentzi	Buthidae	🦂	GFT	C-SBR	N	O
Centruroides margaritatus	Buthidae	🦂🦂	GFT	SB	M	Y
Centruroides vittatus	Buthidae	🦂🦂	G	SCRB	M	Y
Diplocentrus peloncillensis	Diplocentridae	🦂	G	SBR	N	O
Diplocentrus whitei	Diplocentridae	🦂	G	SBR	N	O
Euscorpius flavicaudus	Euscorpiidae	🦂	G	SBR	M	O
Hadogenes bicolor	Ischnuridae	🦂	GR	R	N	Y
Hadogenes troglodytes	Ischnuridae	🦂	GR	R	N	Y
Hadruroides charcasus	Iuridae	🦂?	A	CBR	Y	N
Hadrurus arizonensis	Iuridae	🦂🦂	A	CR	Y	N
Hadrurus spadix	Iuridae	🦂🦂	A	CR	Y	N
Heterometrus cyaneus	Scorpionidae	🦂	FT	SP	Y	N
Heterometrus fulvipes	Scorpionidae	🦂	FT	SP	Y	N
Heterometrus longimanus	Scorpionidae	🦂	FT	SP	Y	N
Heterometrus spinifer	Scorpionidae	🦂	FT	SP	Y	N
Isometrus maculatus	Buthidae	🦂🦂	GT	C-SB	M	O
Opistacanthus asper	Ischnuridae	🦂🦂	DF	B	N	Y
Opistophthalmus ecristatus	Scorpionidae	🦂🦂	AG	C	Y	N
Opistophthalmus glabifrons	Scorpionidae	🦂🦂	AG	C	Y	N
Pandinus cavimanus	Scorpionidae	🦂	FT	SP	Y	N
Pandinus gambiensis	Scorpionidae	🦂	FT	SP	Y	N
Pandinus imperator	Scorpionidae	🦂	FT	SP	Y	N
Pandinus viatoris	Scorpionidae	🦂	FT	SP	Y	N
Paruroctonus boreus	Vaejovidae	🦂	AG	CRB	Y	Y
Scorpio maurus palmatus	Scorpionidae	🦂🦂	A	CR	Y	N
Smeringurus mesaensis	Vaejovidae	🦂	A	C	Y	O
Smeringurus reddelli	Vaejovidae	🦂🦂	G	CRP	N	Y
Uroctonus mordax	Vaejovidae	🦂	DG	CPR	Y	O
Vaejovis carolinianus	Vaejovidae	🦂🦂	GF	SPRB	N	Y
Vaejovis confusus	Vaejovidae	🦂🦂	AG	CRB	M	O
Vaejovis punctatus	Vaejovidae	🦂🦂	AG	CRB	M	O
Vaejovis spinigerus	Vaejovidae	🦂🦂	AG	CRB	Y	O

Communal	Aggressive	Speed	Optimal Temp F°	Optimal Temp C°	Humidity	Mist	When	Water Dish
?	M	M	75±	23.9±	⇒	L	W	Y
Y	N	M	75±	23.9±	⇒	L	4±	Y
Y	M	M	80+	26.7+	⇓-⇒	L	W	Y
N	M	Q	75±	23.9±	⇓	L	0	Y
Y	M	Q	75+	23.9+	M	M	W	Y
Y	M	Q	75+	23.9+	⇒-⇑	L-M	W	Y
Y	M	Q	80±	26.7±	M	L	0	Y
Y	M	Q	80±	26.7±	⇓-M	VL	0	Y
?	N	Q	75±	23.9±	⇒	L-M	W	Y
?	N	Q	75±	23.9	⇒	L-M	W	Y
Y	N	M	75-	23.9-	⇒	L-M	W	Y
N	M	Q	85±	29.4±	⇓	VL	4±	Y
N	M	Q	85±	29.4±	⇓	VL	4±	Y
?	M	M	85±	29.4±	⇓	VL	4±	Y
N	M	M	85+~	29.4+~	⇓	N	N	Y
N	M	M	85+~	29.4+~	D	N	N	Y
Y	M	M	90+	32.2+	⇑	M-H	1-2X	Y
Y	M	M	90+	32.2+	⇑	M-H	1-2X	Y
Y	M	M	90+	32.2+	⇑	M-H	1-2X	Y
Y	M	M	90+	32.2+	⇑	M-H	1-2X	Y
M	M	Q	85±	29.4±	⇒-⇑	M	1X	Y
N	N	M	80+	26.7+	⇒-⇑	M	W	Y
N	M	M	80±	26.7±	⇓	VL	0	Y
N	M	M	80±	26.7±	⇓	VL	0	Y
Y	M	M	85+	29.4+	⇑	M-H	1-2X	Y
Y	M	M	90+	32.2+	⇑	M-H	1-2X	Y
Y	N	M	90+	32.2+	⇑	M-H	1-2X	Y
Y	M	M	90+	32.2+	⇑	M-H	1-2X	Y
N	M	Q	75±~	23.9+~	⇒	M-H	1X	Y
Y	M	Q	85+	29.4+	⇓	N	N	Y
N	V	Q	90±	32.2±	⇓	N	N	Y
M	Y	Q	75±	23±	⇒	M-H	0	Y
N	Y	Q	75+	23.9+	⇑	M-H	1X	Y
Y	N	Q	75±	23.9±	⇒-⇑	M-H	1X	Y
M	N	Q	80±	26.7±	⇓	L	1X	Y
Y	N	Q	80±	26.7±	⇓	L	1X	Y
Y	N	Q	80+	26.7+	⇓	VL	0	Y

HOUSING AND THE IDEAL ENVIRONMENT

The scorpions that are most likely to be kept are found in three basic environments—moist tropical, semi-moist grassland/savanna, and arid desert. Even meager attempts at duplicating their environment will provide suitable caging. Most scorpions are very adaptable and do not require elaborate setups.

Spacious cages are unnecessary and may be detrimental. Most scorpions are ambush predators with very small home ranges, and they may have trouble finding and catching fast, mobile prey (like crickets) in a large cage. A dozen or more of some smaller communal species (e.g., C. vittatus and C. gracilis) can be kept in 15-gallon (57-L) terrariums provided with a surplus of hiding places. They may even breed; however some cannibalism should be expected.

A Secure Home

Scorpions are extremely adept at squeezing through small openings, agile enough to climb an array of objects, and strong enough to lift tops that are considered tight fitting. They are highly capable of escaping. The thought of having a house colonized with scorpions sends

Having taken up residence in an enclosure a Tri-colored Burrowing Scorpion (Opistoph-thalmus ecristatus) waits motionless at the mouth of its burrow for a passing meal.

chills through all but a very few of the most dedicated naturalists.

Prevention and supervision are the best ways to insure safekeeping. The first choices of most keepers are plastic terrariums and glass aquariums. They are widely available and fairly inexpensive, and there is a wide selection of sizes.

The Plastic Cage

Plastic terrariums are produced in sizes and depths to accommodate a variety of small animals and can be bought in any pet shop. The mini ($4^{3}/_{8}$ by $7^{1}/_{8}$ by $5^{1}/_{2}$ inches [$11 \times 18 \times 14$ cm]) will suffice for the smallest species. Small (6 by $9^{1}/_{8}$ by $6^{5}/_{8}$ inches [$15.5 \times 24 \times 18$ cm]) terrariums are an excellent choice for small to mid-sized scorpions, and the larger scorpions do better in medium ($7^{3}/_{4}$ by $11^{3}/_{4}$ by 8 inches [$20 \times 27 \times 21$ cm]) cages. The large sizes are adequate for small community setups, but aquariums are better.

The all-plastic cages have an attractive, one-piece, clear, styrene bottom and sides, and a well-ventilated, tight-fitting top that snaps securely in place. A small, clear styrene door is affixed to the center of the top for safe access. If the slightly angled sides are kept clean, it is almost impossible for a scorpion to climb them.

Nicely conceived and designed, they are good, utilitarian cages for many different types of animals. However, they have a few shortcomings, particularly when used for scorpions. Clear styrene is not as durable as might be assumed. It is easily chipped, broken, and scratched if great care is not taken when cleaning it. Although the top has too many vents to retain much humidity for most scorpions, it is excellent for many arid-living species. Gluing plastic or other material over many of the vented sections is the most practical way to increase humidity.

The Aquarium Cage

Glass sides and bottoms make aquariums heavier and susceptible to cracking. However, they are more rigid and sturdier than styrene cages and will provide years of service. The problem is acquiring a quality, tight-fitting top. Several tops are commercially produced, but they are designed for amphibians, reptiles, and small mammals. Most fit over the outside of the aquarium frame and are held on with a variety of clamping devices. Quite frankly, they are overpriced and fit too loosely, providing gaps that could be exploited by a scorpion. Also, they have an expanse of window screening that prevents maintaining high humidity. Plastic or nylon screening is totally unacceptable; scorpions will rip it with their pincers or "chew" right through it. In fact, some species will do their best to get through aluminum screening.

A Light Source

Although fluorescent light sources are available in different wattages and tube lengths, the compact, one-piece fixture, made for kitchen under-counter use is inexpensive and an excellent size for most cages. Replace the bulb that comes with it with a UV tube (black light), and you will have a light source for unobtrusively observing scorpions. Most home and hardware stores carry the tubes, or they can be ordered. Be sure that you do not mistakenly purchase one of the many bulbs designed for raising plants. Scorpions do not seem to be overly affected by light in the UV spectrum, so they will carry on their nocturnal lives normally.

Alternative Cages

Scorpion keepers with large collections, limited space, and those wanting to do captive breeding have learned to improvise without discomforting the animals or becoming lax on safety. There are literally hundreds of different-size plastic containers that can be easily modified to hold scorpions. The best ones are well made from quality plastic, have tight-fitting, snap-on tops, are stackable, and have maximum ground surface with minimum height.

Small containers are the only way to raise newborn scorpions that need to be kept individually. Plastic deli cups are available in several sizes and have snap-on tops. They are inexpensive, come in a variety of small sizes, and can be bought in quantity from restaurant suppliers or in small numbers from a local restaurant. Rectangular-shaped containers offer more ground surface, require proportionately less shelf space, and their lids are easier to remove. However, they do not come in very small sizes. Housewares and kitchen departments at discount stores stock a variety of containers that will fulfill your needs.

Air and Ventilation

Air and ventilation holes are either drilled or burned into the plastic. An inexpensive soldering pen with a fine point (available at hobby or craft stores) is the near-perfect tool for quickly making three or four holes in dozens of containers. Care must be taken that the orifices are small enough to prevent escapes. This is particularly important if the scorpion gives birth. Many newborns are very small. By making the holes in the sides of the containers, slightly below the top, the containers can be stacked. This efficiently uses shelf space, while permitting air flow.

Air holes drilled into the plastic and covered with aluminum screening (see HOW-TO: Making a Secure Top, p. 62) work well for any of these containers. They should be smaller in diameter, perhaps 1 inch (2.5 cm). One should be drilled in the back above the surface of the substrate and another on the top at the opposite end. This will allow cross ventilation. If they are stacked, the top hole will be obstructed, so three of four additional small holes should be burned into the sides, opposite the back one. This allows for cross ventilation.

Labeling

Many collectors house entire collections in plastic shoe and sweater boxes and food containers. Holes are drilled or burned in them just as those above. Although these containers are not as attractive as aquariums and plastic cages, they are extremely practical and easy to maintain. A plastic label with the scientific name of the animal and a color-coded dot system identifies the contents and goes a long way toward preventing an accident. For instance, a red dot signifies a seriously dangerous scorpion; yellow denotes a quick, flighty one; and green indicates it is innocuous or slow moving.

The Substrate

The material used for burrows is the critical environmental factor for fossorial scorpions. In nature, burrows offer protection from predators and weather, while helping to maintain a constant humidity gradient. Some species spend as much as 90% of their lives in these retreats. Females usually give birth there, with some digging special birthing chambers. Newborns remain in the maternal burrow until their first molt, then disperse and dig their own.

Burrows range from 1–2 inches (2.5–5 cm) to more than 3 feet (1 m) in length, but most are 2–20 inches (5–50 cm). There are exceptions, however. Old, adult *Hadrurus* have been found as deep as 6 feet (2 m) in abandoned rodent tunnels. The type of soil (density, compactness, amount of rock, etc.) determines how far they dig. Some scorpions solve the problem of very hard packed soil or collapsing tunnels by digging under plants or by using existing rodent and lizard burrows.

Substrate for Tropical Scorpions

Choosing an appropriate substrate is a fundamental component in establishing a scorpion's captive environment. Tropical scorpions require high humidity and a damp substrate for burrowing. They will dig burrows, and do well in a mixture of 3 parts potting soil and 1 part cypress mulch. Be sure that the soil does not have added fertilizers or chemicals.

Perlite or vermiculite can be mixed in to help retain water and keep the humidity high. These substances are fine to use because they are natural. Both are found in some potting soil mixes. Perlite is a natural volcanic silicate (glass) that has been greatly expanded by being superheated. Vermiculite is mica that also has been

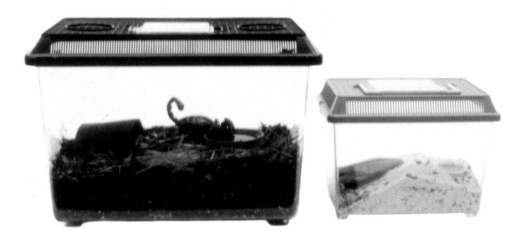

Popular and widely available, plastic terrariums make very good and fairly inexpensive scorpion cages. The larger one, a moist tropical environment, houses a very large Emperor Scorpion (Pandinus imperator), while the smaller one is the arid home to a Black Hairy Scorpion (Hadrurus spadix).

This custom-made aquarium, designed for caging small turtles, was purchased at a large pet shop. The shape provides a maximum surface area with a minimum of height. The top is homemade (see page 62). A dozen Laotian Forest Scorpions (Heterometrus laoticus) were successfully raised in it communally from second instars to near adults.

Several different containers that have been modified to safely hold a variety of scorpion types and sizes. Nearly all are available at home stores. Note the air holes, screening, and labels.

expanded by being heated. The results are light-weight, porous, inert, water-absorbing minerals.

There is an esthetic problem with vermiculite. When wet it tends to stick to the scorpion's exoskeleton. It dries, firmly adhering to the surface, giving the scorpion an unnatural metallic sheen. In many cases it will remain attached until molting. This situation is particularly disturbing if the scorpion is an adult, because it will never shed again.

Regardless of the components of the substrate mixture, before you use it it should be soaked to moisten all the small particles and thoroughly squeezed and partially air-dried until it is just damp. It should not be sopping wet. If an appreciable amount of condensation remains in a few days after the cage cover is in place, the substrate is too wet.

Substrate for Desert Scorpions

Desert scorpions prefer friable, sandy, loamy soils into which they can burrow. A colorful orange sand from Utah *("Jurassic Sand")* has these properties and is sold in many pet shops.

It is fairly expensive (mainly because of packaging and shipping) but may be the perfect substrate if you only have a few scorpions. Mixing it with 25% of other types of sand or potting soil does not dilute its consistency too much.

Pet stores also carry many sizes and colors of sand and gravel for tropical fish. If you prefer colored sand, be certain that it is "colorfast" and truly suitable for fish. No matter where sand is acquired, wash it thoroughly to remove residual chemicals. Beach sand should be avoided because it may contain too much salt.

Basically, all you need is plain old desert sand and gravel. You may be fortunate and find that the sand you have locally is perfect. But be prepared to look elsewhere or improvise to get the consistency that compacts well and does not collapse when it is burrowed into. Be especially careful of where you collect sand. Avoid sand that is close to heavily traveled roads or in areas that may have been sprayed with pesticides or herbicides. Chemical contamination can cause debilitating effects or can be lethal to scorpions.

Dry Mixtures for Burrowing

Bags of clean "play" sand, bought in the building departments of discount, do-it-yourself, and home stores can be used as the basic ingredient, but without additives it does not provide enough consistency for tunneling. Gravel sold in pet stores for use in aquariums is not porous and has a similar consistency. Some keepers use high-quality potting soil, sold as cactus mix.

✔ One method of preparing a desert substrate is to thoroughly mix 1 part fine gravel, 1 part bentonite, and 12–15 parts fine "play" or aquarium grade sands. Bentonite is a natural, porous, very finely powdered aluminum silicate clay used by potters as a binder. It is also used to form the bottoms of naturalistic, outdoor earth-bottomed fish ponds. A small amount of bentonite goes a long way, and too much will scratch and excessively wear the exoskeleton. It can be bought at some art supply stores, particularly those that cater to potters and ceramic artists.

✔ Another good mixture (particularly for scorpions that live in less arid conditions) is 5 parts of quality potting soil with 10 parts of sand, and 1 part bentonite to make it firmer. A few parts of finely chopped cypress mulch can be included to thicken the soil mix.

Ceramic makers have an amazing number of additional sand and clay products at their disposal. Grog is recycled, previously fired clay that has been crushed and ground into different thicknesses. Medium or coarse grades blend nicely with sand and bentonite to add texture and binding ability. As a precaution, a painter's mask should be worn when mixing any finely ground silica sands or compounds.

None of these percentages or methods is foolproof, and a little experimenting may be needed to provide the perfect substrate for a particular scorpion.

As a preventative measure, wet and microwave the substrate for several minutes in a microwave oven (high setting) to kill any microorganisms. Ten or fifteen minutes in a regular oven at 350°F (175°C) will probably do just as well.

Place the well-blended mixture in the cage. Thoroughly wet and put it into a compacted state. Allow it to dry completely, and add the furnishings and water dish. Be sure that it is dry before introducing the scorpions.

Starting a Burrow

A scorpion can be induced to dig a burrow in a predetermined spot if a short section of tunnel entrance has been provided. Use a pencil to make a hole in the soil large enough to accommodate the scorpion. The burrow should have a moisture gradient, ranging from a dry surface to a somewhat damp portion toward the deepest part of the substrate. The upper soil should be kept dry to prevent caking on the scorpion's tarsi and for ease in initiating a burrow.

A trick for retaining a moisture gradient: One way to achieve this is to only moisten the lowest reaches of the substrate.

1. Cover the bottom of the cage with .5 inch (1.3 cm) of medium gravel and add the substrate.

2. Cut the ends of a few drinking straws at an angle, and push them vertically into the soil until they touch the cage bottom. Cut them off so that they protrude 1 inch (2.5 cm) or so above the surface. Plastic straws are more rigid and last longer than paper straws.

3. Periodically, pour a very small amount of water into the opening. It will migrate to the bottom. Placing the nozzle of a spray bottle directly in the hole will avoid spillage and wetting the surface. The amount of water must be minimal, just enough to moisten the very bottom sand. The gravel layer acts as a reservoir.

Capillary action will spread the water upward, creating a gradient. Ideally, the scorpions will dig to the depth they prefer. The number of straws is determined by the size of the cage. There is less chance of the scorpions digging them up if they are placed along the cage periphery. A fairly even water level will be maintained in a large cage if a few straws are inserted away from the edges. A similar effect can be achieved by using a plastic, bendable straw. Insert the straw along the periphery, bend it at a right angle, and bury it with the opening facing the cage's center. Great care must be taken that the amount of moisture is minimal and maintained at a fairly constant but very low level.

Substrate for Other Scorpions

Most other scorpions (grassland/savanna) can be kept in a soil that is a mixture of materials. Small cypress bark chips or mulch, peat moss, and pieces of sphagnum moss will "thicken" the substrate, while sand will make it more friable. Until you become an advanced scorpion keeper and can better evaluate their qualities and potential hazards, avoid using the exotic substrates sold for reptiles, amphibians, and other animals. Do not use mulches containing cedar, pine, ground sugarcane, or the treated, aromatic ones claiming to maintain a "fresh" environment; some are lethal to arachnids.

A Commercial Substrate Additive with Promise

One product that has been used successfully by several arachnid keepers is ground, dehy-

drated coconut shell. It is sold as a pet substrate and as a potting soil additive for gardeners. When soaked in hot water, the densely compressed brick expands to several times its mass. It not only holds moisture very well (which makes it excellent for *Pandinus* and *Heterometrus*), but it also mixes with other materials to make them moisture retentive, friable, and "thick" enough to prevent burrows from collapsing.

Some "fine tuning" will be necessary because a scorpion's moisture needs vary greatly. Also, there is very little if any information about the needs of many taxa that are periodically available. As a result, trial and error may be the only way to provide a suitable captive environment. Because the amount of moisture is important, it should never be disregarded.

A test for a scorpion's moisture needs: Temporarily supply a larger cage than is necessary—twice the size is perfect. Prepare consistent substrate and furnishings throughout the cage. Increase the moisture content of the soil at one end, while leaving the other end drier. The straw system works well with desert taxa, and misting may be needed for tropical or grassland forms. If several specimens are available, it may be useful to experiment with a variety of substrate mixtures as well. Continue the procedure, and within a week or so, the scorpion will have chosen its preferred environment. The scorpion should then be moved into a smaller cage that provides its optimum living conditions.

A scorpion's actions will provide additional clues to its needs. If it spends a great deal of time on its water dish, it probably needs a moister substrate or higher humidity. If it sits off the substrate on top of its furnishings, it may need to be kept drier.

Cage Furnishings

Pet dealers have a variety of naturalistic retreats that are specially designed for small reptiles and invertebrates. Some have built-in water dishes. Thoroughly wash everything you add to the cage to remove any residue it may be carrying, including soap. Placing them in a microwave oven for a few minutes is an effective method to dry and sterilize furnishings.

Flat rocks: Flat rocks can be stacked and glued together with silicone aquarium cement to form safe crevices for Flat-rock and other lithophilic scorpions. A scorpion's flattened shape is a clue that it prefers tight spaces and is more secure when it is in contact with the top and sides of its hiding place.

Plastic containers and fixtures: Although not esthetically pleasing, inverted small, shallow, opaque, plastic food containers, with entrances cut into them, work well. With a little thought and improvisation, you will find many things that will do the job. Several different sizes of plastic plumbing fixtures partially buried into the substrate can be used as tunnels and burrow entrances. A light sanding (medium grade sandpaper) of the inside walls reduces the smooth texture, permitting a better foothold.

Peat moss retreats: Garden shops carry inexpensive, lightweight seed starter pots made from compressed peat moss. If they are cut in half lengthwise, they make excellent retreats for most scorpions. They have a natural look, come in several sizes, and retain moisture very well. A light, weekly spraying on their outer surface helps. They are excellent moisture-retaining retreats for scorpions that are undergoing a molt.

Water

The very small clay or plastic dishes used under flower pots are good water dishes for larger scorpions. Plastic medicine bottle tops are serviceable small water receptacles. In fact, any plastic bottle top can be used effectively. Placing some gravel in the water will prevent

A bookcase used for holding a variety of cages housing more than 100 scorpions of various sizes and species. Heat tapes are affixed to the back wall of each shelf to supply auxiliary heat.

A battery-driven, very accurate, digital thermometer combined with a humidity sensor and an inexpensive stick-on thermometer (for plants and fish).

food animals from drowning. A small piece of sponge serves the same function and also helps maintain humidity. It must be kept scrupulously clean and changed frequently to prevent unhealthy conditions. A water dish with a wider surface area will evaporate more water, raising the humidity. Placing a small one in a retreat is a great way to keep the humidity level elevated.

Ventilation

Ventilation is also important for your scorpion. Covering the entire top of a cage with a sheet of glass or plastic should not be done. Even if high humidity is required, there should always be some air movement to remove stale air and to prevent mold. The simplest way is to place vents at opposite ends of the cage. (See discussion on page 50.) Larger vents are important to keep desert environments dry.

Temperature

Desert and tropical scorpions require warm temperatures (80–95°F [26.7–32.2°C]) to feed, digest, and grow normally, whereas those from temperate regions will do well at room temperature (70–78°F [21.1–25.6°C]). If your scorpions need high temperatures, heating the entire

room may be the best alternative. Hot air rises, so place scorpions that prefer slightly cooler temperatures close to the floor, and those preferring warmer ones higher, toward the ceiling.

A large closet or cabinet is another way to control temperatures. Many auxiliary heat sources with built-in thermostats work well. If the room cannot be easily heated, individual heat sources should be used. Caution must be taken to always ensure maximum safety when using any heating device.

Heat Tapes

Many heating products that have been designed for reptiles are usable for arachnids as well. The best of these are the 3-inch

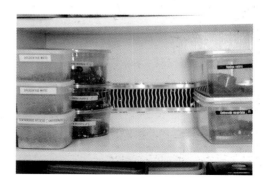

A heat tape can be seen affixed to the back wall of the bookcase unit seen on the previous page. Each shelf has its own tape.

(7.6-cm) and 10-inch (25.4-cm) wide, paper thin, plastic heat tapes. They are designed to spread heat over the entire surface, preventing one area from getting too hot. Narrower tapes work well with nearly all cages, whereas the wider ones are better suited for very large enclosures. They can be bought by the linear foot, and cut to the desired length. Electrical connections are straightforward and simple, but may require adult supervision to be completely safe. Many sources sell the tapes precut to your specifications and fully wired.

The tape should be placed either under one end of the cage bottom or affixed to the back wall of the shelf on which the cage is located. These positions serve three functions: the tape remains outside the cage, it is a precaution against overheating, and it enables the scorpion to move away from the heat source, seeking its own temperature gradient. Many keepers believe that placing the heat source under the cage is not good because scorpions innately burrow to escape the heat, and this provides the opposite effect. Affixing the heat tape to the back wall avoids this problem. Water dishes placed closer to the heat source increase evaporation and humidity.

Other heating devices: Radiant heat bulbs, "hot rocks," and other in-cage heaters can become too hot, and there is the ever-present electric wire that must be brought into the cage. Many European keepers like using a dangling red bulb of wattage proportionate to the size of the cage for heat. The red light is not perceived by scorpions and does not seem to affect their activities. Here again, however, there is the electric cord problem. Advanced keepers with larger collections should investigate all the heating supplies made for reptile hobbyists.

Thermometers

Plastic strip thermometers that stick on an aquarium wall are an excellent way to monitor cage temperature. They are so inexpensive that every cage should have one. Place it level with the substrate, near the warmest part of the cage. Sensitive, battery-operated, digital thermometers are available at electronics stores. They can be read in Fahrenheit and centigrade, have a low and high memory, and record the temperature at its location, as well as the temperature at the end of the remote-sensing probe.

Other versions have a digital thermometer and humidity gauge, but no remote probe. Placing one inside a cage shows the temperature and humidity accurately. It is particularly useful to calculate the amount of water that is necessary to achieve a constant percentage of humidity.

Cannibalism and the Communal Tank

Cannibalism is a way of life—or should I say way of death?—for scorpions. As aggressive predators they see any small, moving creature as a meal and react accordingly. However, there are situations when they do not attack.

It appears that certain chemical and tactile sensors block the initial attack reaction. As we will see later, a mother will not eat her newborns, but may have no qualms about consuming the babies of others. She seems to identify her own by smell and touch.

Some species can live communally without eating conspecifics. But, if a member of another species enters the territory, it is just another food animal. In some situations, communal feeding may occur.

Most scorpions live by themselves and will eat a scorpion that wanders by. A few are predominantly nomadic and cannibalistic, seeking out and eating any suitable invertebrate, including another scorpion.

Communal Species

It is not known why some scorpions can live rather tranquilly in communal groups whereas others are fierce adversaries. There are still other groups that tolerate neighbors, but maintain and protect territories. This likely has to do with the prevalence of food, limited proper habitat, and small home range. Some species are very aggressive predators.

Although some keepers have been able to house different species together, regardless of how nonaggressive they may be, it seems to be taunting fate. In the wild, few taxa have been found living in close proximity. If you choose to try mixing species in a cage, food must be given to them at least once a week so that they are always adequately fed. The scorpions should be all approximately the same size and more than enough hiding places should be provided throughout the cage. A water dish should be available at all times. And finally, the size of the cage is important. The size of a cage limits the range of a species forcing the inhabitants to live within predetermined and human-induced boundaries. At times, this situation becomes stressful and cannibalism may occur. Females may live together for years, but suddenly one will attack and kill another without obvious provocation.

Surface area: The amount of surface area is usually the important factor. Arboreal scorpions, like many Bark Scorpions, can be kept communally in a tall cage with limited ground area, provided there are vertical places affording numerous small cracks and crevices in which they can hide. A hollow section of palm tree trunk, curls of cork bark, or the basal sections of attached epiphytes are near-perfect microhabitats. Augment the vertical surface by covering the floor with a 3-inch (7.5-cm) layer of moistened cypress mulch and as many as 10 adults will live amicably in a tall 15-gallon (57-L) aquarium.

Although dozens of gregarious ground dwellers, like Emperor Scorpions and Forest Scorpions, are frequently seen at pet shops heaped together in a 20-gallon (76-L) aquarium, those conditions are terribly overcrowded. Four to six equally sized specimens, preferably two or three pairs, are appropriate for a cage with that amount of floor area. The substrate should be at least 3 inches (7.6 cm) of a moist, tropical soil mixture, and a half dozen 6–10-inch (15–25-cm) pieces of cork bark should be strewn about the surface as retreats. A large shallow water dish completes the furnishings.

The Israeli Gold Scorpion (*S. maurus palmatus*) is a small communal desert species. Six (again preferably three pairs) can safely live in a 10-gallon (38-L) aquarium. A 3–5-inch (7.6–12.7-cm) layer of a friable, sandy desert mixture is a good substrate. A few flat stones, pieces of weathered wood, or cork bark placed on the surface provides the scorpions with additional hiding places. Some scorpions prefer to make scrapes, so include flat objects large enough for them to make scrapes under. A water dish should be provided.

Handling

As stated previously, there are no reasons for free-handling scorpions. However, there are

An Arizona Hairy Scorpion (**Hadrurus arizonensis**) *safely hides in one of the chambers of burrows it dug.*

quick spurts and not stop at the end of a table. If a scorpion falls to the floor uninjured, it will run for the nearest dark place. This may be an incredibly small spot that is inaccessible, like an air conditioning duct opening, under a large piece of furniture, or under a major appliance.

When removing a scorpion from its cage, place the cage in a larger container, eliminating an immediate place of escape. Plastic sweater or blanket boxes hold smaller cages, and a sink or bathtub is an excellent place for larger ones. Be sure to block the drain.

Forceps

In emergency situations and tight spaces, rubber-tipped forceps are the tool of choice. A pair should always be kept within easy reach of your scorpions. Special, 6- and 10-inch, rubber-tipped forceps are available from some pet shops or by mail order. The soft rubber tips allow a firm grip on the smooth, hard surface of the exoskeleton and help prevent injury. The same cushioning effect can be accomplished by placing short sections of tight-fitting, clear, neoprene tubing over an ordinary forceps' metal tips. The airline hose used with aquarium air pumps is perfect for this.

times when they must be moved or transported. The best, safest, and least-stressful method is scooping. A large soup ladle is the perfect implement for catching all but the biggest scorpions. The animal is scooped up with a quick, direct sweep, or very gently prodded into the spoon with a pencil, soda straw, small artist's paintbrush, or similar implement. Larger scorpions and those that are to be moved more than a few feet are best scooted into a plastic container and secured with a lid (like a deli cup).

It is important to be cautious when working with scorpions. Scorpions are prone to move in

A large female Emperor Scorpion (**Pandinus imperator**) *drinking from its water dish. Note the moist mulch substrate and the halved, peat moss seed starter cup being used as a hide.*

*A large communal cage with a thriving,
breeding colony of Slenderbrown Bark
Scorpions (Centruroides gracilis) in the
author's living room.*

*Ten-inch long rubber-tipped forceps are
being used to move a potentially dangerous
Mozambique Fat-tailed Scorpion
(Parabuthus mossambicensis).*

Great care should be exercised when handling scorpions with forceps. Grip it by a metasomal segment; preferably by the segment directly before the telson, and quickly lift it above the substrate. The pressure should be just firm enough to hold the animal, but not to injure it. There is a fine line here to prevent external or internal injury, and practice is needed to perfect the technique. Be prepared for the scorpion to react by forcefully grabbing the forceps with its pincers. This is not a safe way of picking up robust species because their weight exerts a great amount of strain on their metasomas. Because it is so stressful for all scorpions, it is not the preferred method. However, it frequently is the only way to grab an escaping scorpion. A small aquarium fishnet is a handy and safe way to cover a scorpion. Sliding a thin piece of cardboard under the net will simplify entrapping and transporting it. The scorpion's legs and/or pedipalps will usually become ensnared in the mesh, so the release must be done with caution.

Because of their diminutive size and obvious fragility, tiny, newborn, and recently molted scorpions should never be grabbed with forceps. Scooping with a container or fishnet is the safest method of handling all scorpions.

More About Handling

Leather gloves can be used to grab medium and larger scorpions, but the thickness of the leather prevents feeling the amount of pressure being exerted. Although welder's gloves are frequently used to handle small venomous snakes, large tarantulas, and small feisty mammals that are prone to bite or scratch, they are much too thick and cumbersome for scorpions.

The best alternative to the commercially available aquarium top is to make your own. Your local hardware or home center carries all the materials you'll need, and it is a lot simpler than you might expect.

Most aquariums produced today are all glass with a molded plastic top and bottom frame for appearance, rigidity, and to prevent the corners from chipping. A small lip on the inside edge of the top plastic frame is meant to hold a glass cover but it is also perfect for holding your homemade fit-in top.

There are two designs for easy-to-build fit-in tops—aluminum window screens and a modified sheet of acrylic/plastic. Many variations are possible by combining the two concepts. With some thought, you will likely produce a style that best fits your particular need.

A Screen Top

Using a few simple tools and preformed parts, it is easy to fabricate aluminum window screen covers. The materials (aluminum screening, aluminum frame rails, plastic corner pieces, and soft plastic beading) are inexpensive and are available in hardware and do-it-yourself stores.

1. Measure the dimension on the inside lip of the plastic aquarium top. Account for the size of the plastic corners, and cut the side rails with a hacksaw or small handsaw.

2. Snap the rails together with corner pieces, and you will have a frame that is square and rigid.

3. Cut the aluminum screening with a sharp knife or scissors, press in place, and secure it with the special plastic beading with a wheeled pizza-cutter-like tool made specifically for the job.

4. Trim the excess, and the top is finished.

A one-piece screen top is most suitable for desert cages because it does not retain moisture well, but higher humidity is required for other species. A sheet of 1/8-inch (3-mm) acrylic plastic will solve that problem. Turn the top over, measure, and cut a piece of plastic to fit snugly between the two long sides, being careful to leave spaces at either short end for ventilation. A 1-inch (2.5-cm) opening is adequate.

Run a bead of silicone aquarium adhesive approximately 1/2 inch (1.3 cm) from the edge, along the entire periphery of the plastic and add a few additional dabs to maintain a bond with the screening toward the center. Let it dry for 10 minutes, until it is tacky. With the adhesive side up, turn the screen top over and carefully align and press the screening into the plastic. Make sure the plastic fits properly between the long sides. The bond should be tight. Let is set for a few hours. Then turn it over, plastic side up, and apply a very fine bead of silicone along the entire edge of the plastic, making a clean smooth edge. Let it dry and cure for a day or two. The acetic acid odor

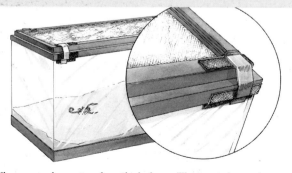

The screened cage top described above. The inset shows the Velcro closure.

SECURE TOP

will eventually evaporate. To assure a firm closure, small straps of Velcro should be attached at strategic spots along the edge.

An Acrylic/Plastic Top

Although acrylic/plastic tops are not as attractive and professional looking as the screen types, they are simpler to construct, less expensive, and efficient. For aquariums up to 10 gallons (38 L), two sheets of ⅛-inch (3-mm) plastic material are cut to snuggly fit the inside lip of the top. The use of a fine-toothed saw or very sharp matte knife will ensure a clean edge. Temporarily tape the two sheets together along the edges.

The materials, tools, and techniques for building an acrylic top.

1. Choose and mark a location at opposite ends of the fit-in top, and drill a 1–2.5-inch (2.5–6.4-cm) hole completely through the stacked sheets using a circular hole saw. These saws come in several sizes (usually as a stacked kit), and are made for installing door locks. If the bit is allowed to cut through the plastic slowly and not forced, it will not crack the acrylic. A little light sanding will smooth the edges. The size and number of holes varies with the dimensions of the aquarium and the amount of ventilation desired. Some air movement is necessary, but the amount of evaporation must be considered as well.

2. Sandwich aluminum window screening between the mated plastic sheets and roughly trim the excess. Apply a thick bead of silicone adhesive to one sheet, carefully following the outside edge surrounding the holes, with an indent of ½ inch (12.7 mm). Dabs of silicone should be randomly added to the inside expanse of plastic to ensure a consistent bond. Press the screening into it. Add a thin bead of the adhesive onto the screening, carefully matching the previous beads as much as possible. Align and press the second sheet to produce firm contact. To be sure that the edges are even, place a weight evenly across the entire surface, and allow the silicone to cure for at least 24 hours (preferably for a few days). The acetic acid odor will eventually dissipate. When the silicone is dry, carefully trim the excess screening with a sharp matte knife, being certain no wire protrudes.

3. Attach a miniature cabinet pull toward the center of the front edge as a handle to help lift the lid. Black or opaque plastic presents a better appearance, because it hides the cement and excess screening, and it prevents the passage of light. Because the plastic flexes easily, thicker material, ¼ inch (6.4 mm) or ⅜ inch (10 mm), will be needed to make tops for larger aquariums. Place small Velcro tabs along the top, as was done above, to hold the top securely.

A quicker-to-assemble version can be made from a single piece of ¼-inch (6.4-mm) plastic. However, they are less stable and will warp in time. Simply drill the appropriate vent holes and glue patches of screening to cover them. Although a hot glue gun will do an adequate job, silicone adhesive forms a more permanent bond.

FOOD AND FEEDING

When compared to the way other animals eat, scorpions are bizarre. Food is predigested before it is sucked into the body. As unusual as it seems, predigestion is not unique to scorpions; many other arachnids also do it.

The Mechanics of Feeding

Prey is grabbed by the pincers and brought to the mouth. It may be killed first or eaten alive, depending on how much it struggles. The chelicerae, which resemble and function like small scissors, have cutting surfaces that tear and grind the prey animal into minute pieces and pass the pastelike food into the preoral cavity.

Food pieces are mixed with digestive juices in the preoral cavity and strained by a pair of maxillary brushes (each is an oval-shaped grouping of tiny, rigid bristles) to remove indigestible parts. Brushes contain chemoreceptors that have an unknown function, but likely discern different chemicals providing a primitive form "taste." In addition, they are used to groom the pedipalps and legs. Matted debris is discharged, while the liquefied food is sucked into the gut.

Further digestion and absorption occur in the gut. The mesosoma can distend noticeably, enabling a massive intake of food. Nutrients are slowly digested and absorbed over a period

*A close-up of an **Opistacanthus asper** eating a cricket.*

of days; how quickly depends on the ambient temperature. Higher temperatures expedite the process. Feces, an almost dry, chalky, white substance containing mostly guanine and uric acid, is passed from the anus.

Feeding Strategies

Scorpions are opportunistic predators that use two strategies to procure food: ambushing and foraging. Each has its benefits and drawbacks.

Ambushing

Fossorial scorpions spend most of their lives within or near their burrows and are ambush predators. They move to the hidden entrances of their burrows at dusk and sit-and-wait, their pincers open, poised, ready to snare any luckless passing meal. Most ambush predators crush their prey and use venom sparingly, if at all. Food may be consumed where it is captured or taken into the burrow and eaten. Ambush predation is efficient, expending very little energy. Also, it is a relatively safe hunting strategy, preventing the scorpion from becoming the prey of other carnivores.

Foraging

On the other hand, forager's tactics expend much energy, and, because the scorpion leaves the protection of its hiding place and actively searches for food, it faces more inherent risks than those that ambush. Foragers are smaller, quicker, climb more freely, and have fairly potent venom. Because they are on the move so much, they may encounter other scorpions, which they will eat or possibly be eaten by. The Giant Sand Scorpion, *Smeringurus mesaensis,* of the southwestern United States is known for its cannibalistic tendencies. Most of its diet consists of other scorpions, including its own species.

At least one Devil Scorpion, *Tityus fasciolatus,* and another South American scorpion genus, *Armitermes,* live in termite mounds. The proximity of such a large food source makes procuring it very simple; the scorpions move around within the mound, stop at a likely spot, and pick off termites as they walk by. As long as the mound remains viable, a colony of scorpions could live and reproduce for generations, without having to leave its confines.

A Balanced Diet

A hungry scorpion will eat almost anything small enough for it to grab and kill. However, there seems to be a high-end and a low-end size preference. Logically, larger scorpions eat larger food items than smaller ones. In fact, bigger scorpions have trouble catching small prey. Scorpions with large chela can subdue and hold large prey. The favored prey size for most species, however, appears to be one-third that of the scorpion. It is unusual for a scorpion to take an item more than two-thirds its body size; half or slightly less is usually the upper limit. In fact, many scorpions will run away from prey that is too large. During times when prey is abundant, insects with thick, hard exoskeletons and those that produce repugnant chemicals are commonly refused (e.g., few scorpions eat wood lice).

Crickets and mealworms are the main choice for captive scorpions. They are available from many sources, inexpensive, and easy to rear and maintain. With few exceptions, they are more than adequate food animals for nearly all scorpions. The scorpion's low metabolism (allowing low energy consumption) and the ability to consume large meals enable it to fast for long periods.

Feast or famine feeding combined with seasonal changes in temperature and humidity, which necessitate periods of prolonged rest (hibernation and aestivation), are relevant for a scorpion's long-term survival. Also, regulating food intake to ensure that there are "lean" periods will prevent the unhealthy equivalent of obesity. These strategies should be used as part of captive husbandry to ensure a healthy animal.

Some Undesirables

Most pest insects, such as ants and cockroaches, can be used as food; however, they may have potential drawbacks. Their social habits, size, and potential for causing unwanted infestations make them problematic food animals. Certain social insects, bees in particular, have been used as food. Commercially available wax worms, *Galleria mellonella,* are fed to many kinds of insect-eating animals, but many scorpions refuse them. Also, they are extremely soft-bodied and tend to ooze freely while being killed and eaten, leaving a sticky mess that may attract dangerous mites.

When and How Much Food

A fallacy that has been circulated for many years is that if you feed a scorpion as much as it will eat it will continue to eat, gorging itself to death. A hungry scorpion can eat a tremendous amount of food, so much so that it may indeed gorge itself until its mesosoma is so swollen that it appears as though it will bust. However, when sated, it will stop and go into hiding to digest. If kept at its optimum temperature the scorpion will digest this meal, defecate, and in a few days to a week feed again. Or it may refuse to eat for some time, perhaps several months. Healthy adult males are notorious for undertaking long fasts.

Although the amount of food given per feeding is arbitrary, it should be monitored and guided by concern for the animal's welfare. It is dependent on the physical condition of the scorpion, the temperature at which it is being kept, and its age. A healthy scorpion will have good body weight and not appear either gaunt or pudgy. Higher temperatures cause rapid metabolism, which requires additional food for the scorpion to maintain its weight.

Because they are growing constantly, young scorpions will eat as much as they can, frequently to the point of being gluttonous. They should be well fed, perhaps a few small crickets every 3 days, but not to the point of being continuously bloated.

Types of Food

In addition to crickets (see HOW-TO: Raising Food Items, page 70), scorpions can subsist on a diet of various other insects.

Mealworms *(Tenebrio molitor):* Mealworms, the larvae of a species of Darkling Beetle, are an old standby food. They range in size from .25 to .75 inch (6.4–10 mm) in length. Millions are raised as food for amphibians, lizards, birds, and small mammals.

Mealworms are extremely easy to rear, and every scorpion keeper should have a colony or two as a backup food supply. They can be useful in winter months when crickets are difficult to acquire. Plastic shoeboxes and sweater boxes make excellent rearing containers because mealworms and the adult beetles do not climb well. Although bran is the food of choice, oats and other cereal grains will work.

Buy 1,000 or 2,000 mealworms from a mail-order supplier. They are really inexpensive in quantity (2,000 is the normal minimum and costs approximately $15 including shipping). Feed off as many as you need, there will be plenty. Incidentally, if needed, they can be kept for months in a closed container in the least-cold section of a refrigerator, probably the vegetable drawer.

Setting up a culture is incredibly easy. Dump a few dozen of the larvae into a container with 3 inches (7.4 cm) of bran, add a piece of potato, carrot, squash, apple (sliced in half lengthwise), or a cabbage leaf for moisture. Cover it with a few layers of newspaper or paper towel and put it aside in a warm, dark spot. Replace the moist food source when it dries or is consumed. If kept at room temperature, the mealworms will metamorphose into beetles, and the adults lay eggs, starting a new cycle. All phases should be seen in a month or two, and you can start to harvest.

The mealworms (larvae) will gather in the paper or can be sifted from the bran with a small, kitchen strainer. Any size mealworm can be used as food for your scorpions. Leave the pupae and adults to renew the colony. Every 6 months sift the grain, discard the dry, powdery feces that have collected on the bottom, and place the remaining animals in fresh bran. Raw bran can be bought in health food stores by the

A large Emperor Scorpion (**Pandinus imperator**) *makes a meal of an unfortunate Sphaerodactylid Gecko.*

A Black Hairy Scorpion (**Hadrurus spadix**) *eating a Giant Mealworm* (**Zoophobias morio**) *head first.*

pound. If more than a few dozen adults are in a culture, they should be discarded or used to start new cultures. They will eat their eggs if the container is too crowded. Unfortunately, most scorpions will not eat the adults, and the pupae do not move enough to be recognized as food.

Super Mealworms *(Zoophobas morio):* Recently, larvae of another Darkling Beetle, super mealworms, have become available. These larvae eat rotting wood and sawdust and are several times larger (1.5–2 inches [3.8–5.1 cm]) and bulkier than regular mealworms. These robust larvae of a tropical beetle have strong chewing mouthparts and are capable of inflicting painful, possibly damaging, bites on small amphibians and lizards. They are known to chew their way out of plastic deli cups. They are no threat to mid-sized and larger scorpions.

Super mealworms are not cold tolerant and are more difficult and time consuming to breed than regular mealworms. Nearly all that I have seen for sale are full-sized larvae, and they are

much cheaper if purchased in large quantities. They can be kept as healthy larvae for up to 2 months in a plastic tub containing sawdust kept between 60 and 70°F (15.6–21.1°C). They will perish at 50°F (10°C) or lower. As a precaution, be sure that you are getting *Zoophobas;* there are hormone-treated *Tenebrio molitor* that are almost as large, but have thick exoskeletons that are difficult to digest.

Fruit Flies (*Drosophila* spp.): Wingless and vestigial winged fruit flies are tiny, mutant forms of normally winged flies that are cultured for use in genetics experiments and as live tropical fish food. Their small size (⅛ inch [3.2 mm]) makes them an excellent food for newborn and very small scorpions. Two species, *Drosophila melanogaster,* and the slightly larger *Drosophila hydei,* are obtainable from mail order from biological supply houses and a number of professional *Drosophila* breeders. It is best to start by buying a complete rearing kit that includes bottles, sponge stoppers, culture

This gluttonous behavior is typical of a hungry scorpion in times when food is available. Here an Emperor Scorpion (Pandinus imperator) *has a cricket in its pincer and another one is being eaten.*

medium, starter flies, and instructions. Although near-perfect in size for most very young scorpions, *D. hydei* readily climb and spend most of their time on the underside of the scorpion container's lid, out of reach of most scorpions.

Roaches (*Blatella, Periplaneta,* and *Blatta*): Three common kinds of roaches—the German Cockroach *(Blatella germanica),* the American Cockroach *(Periplaneta americana),* and the Oriental Cockroach *(Blatta orientalis)*—are eaten by some of the larger scorpions. Roaches have a distinct odor, and unlike tarantulas, many scorpions refuse them. Even though the Malagasy Giant Hissing Roaches *(Grompha-dorhina portentosa)* are widely available as "pets," adults are huge, much too large for most scorpions. However, if the scorpions will eat them, immatures are an excellent nutrient source.

One taxon, *Blaberus craniiferus,* is available occasionally from scientific suppliers. They cannot fly and are poor climbers. Take extra care that any container for roaches has a tight-fitting cover as a precaution.

A red light source should be used for heat, because roaches are nocturnal, and additional scrap vegetable matter will help limit the amount of more expensive dry foods. They can climb almost anything, so great care must be taken to contain them. Applying a thin band of petroleum jelly around the container, slightly below the top, will help keep them in.

All roaches are easy to breed. They can be kept basically the same way as crickets (see page 70). Although debatable, the parasites and bacteria carried in the guts of wild-caught roaches could be harmful to the animals that prey on them.

The three development stages of a Giant Mealworm (Zoophobas morio) *after hatching. From left to right: the larvae (mealworm), the pupae, and the adult. Scorpions will usually only eat the larval stage.*

HOW-TO: RAISING FOOD

If you only keep a few scorpions, it probably is not worth raising many kinds of food. It is more sensible to buy crickets when they are needed. Pet shops and bait stores are good local sources. Read the advertisements in reptile or aquarium magazines for other food animal sources. The Young Entomologist's Society's publication edited by Gary Dunn, *Caring for Insect Livestock: An Insect Rearing Manual,* is an excellent, inexpensive source of information regarding maintaining and breeding a wide variety of arthropods.

Any wooded lot will provide an adequate assortment of edible insects (e.g., grubs, beetles, grasshoppers, crickets, butterflies, and moths), especially during the warmer months. Be aware, however, that urban populations may be carrying a high pesticide and chemical load. When maintaining live foods, good housekeeping and cleanliness are paramount. Excess moisture can be a problem because it promotes mold and mites. Both are detrimental to a scorpion's health. Adequate ventilation in all cages helps reduce the moisture problem.

House Crickets
(Acheta domestica)

Because of their diet, crickets contain a wide variety of vitamins, proteins, and minerals, and they can be easily "gut loaded." "Gut loading" is nothing more than feeding an enriched diet to crickets before they are offered as food. This passes on extra nutrients and has proved to be an effective method of improving the diets of vertebrates. It is particularly good for adding calcium, but its nutritive value for arachnids is unknown. Crickets should be healthy, well fed, and given water before using them as food.

Crickets can be purchased in many sizes from newborn ("pinheads") to adults. To save money, buy a quantity (1,000 cost less than $20, including shipping) of a smaller size and raise them toward adulthood. They grow at slightly different rates, so a variety of sizes are available at any given time. Pinheads take 6 weeks to reach adulthood, and adults live approximately 2 weeks.

If you can allot the space, accept some odor, handle the chirping, and will spend a few hours a month maintaining them, crickets are relatively simple to breed and extremely prolific. Aside from food, two things are required: a constant supply of clean water and a heat source. Sexing crickets is easy, adult males "chirp" and females have long median ovipositors.

A very large, deep, smooth-sided container is necessary to maintain a thriving colony. Two or three containers that have been started at different

A container for keeping crickets. Note the screened ventilation holes in the top.

times provide a continuous supply of all sizes. The simplest container is a plastic storage bin. Most home and discount stores carry them in 18 gallon (46 L) and larger sizes. It must be at least 16 inches (41 cm) deep to prevent the crickets from jumping out. If the upper few inches of the deepest containers are kept scrupulously clean, they cannot crawl out. The least-complex preventative method is a screened top. Aside from keeping them from escaping, it permits excellent air circulation.

Add .5–.75 inch (1.3–1.9 mm) of clean, dry peat or sand and several egg cartons or the cardboard tubes from paper towels or toilet paper as hiding places. When crowded, crickets will become stressed, cannibalistic, and suffocate each other.

Many kinds of crushed dry dog, cat, rodent, or other pet foods are good choices as food for crickets.

Specially formulated cricket food is available, but small quantities are expensive. Unmedicated chicken-laying mash is an excellent, inexpensive food; however, it is difficult to locate in urban areas. It is sold in large quantities, but occasionally can be bought by the pound. Be certain it is not medicated. The medicinal additives will destroy the natural flora in the crickets' guts, disturb the digestive balance, and likely kill them.

Scrap fruits and vegetables can be offered for nutritional and water content. Crickets dehydrate rapidly, so a water reservoir, available from pet stores and mail-order cricket suppliers, must be accessible and filled at all times. A safely installed dangling lightbulb, of a size that will produce enough heat to maintain a temperature near 85°F (29.4°C), is needed for optimum production.

When properly cared for, crickets breed readily. Place a plastic container at least 6 inches

A simple method of maintaining a breeding colony of mealworms (see page 67). Note the ventilation holes in the top.

(15.2 cm) in diameter with 1 inch (2.5 cm) of clean, damp (not soaking) sand or vermiculite in with adult crickets, and they will start to lay eggs almost immediately. If the substrate container is slightly sloped, excess moisture will drain toward the lower end.

Remove the container after a day or two and place it inside a covered plastic sweater box with a fine layer of dry sand covering the bottom. Keep it warm and check the dampness of the sand in the egg-bearing container every few days, and mist it lightly if it is drying noticeably. Do not overwater; it should not be noticeably wet, just damp. In 2 weeks, hundreds of pinhead crickets will emerge. They can be fed the finely mashed food used for adults. A water dish, with either gravel or a sponge protruding above the surface, will provide water and avert drowning. It must always contain water.

As the crickets grow, move them into a large container and feed and water them as suggested for adults. In about 6 weeks, they reach adulthood and the cycle starts over again. Change the substrate every month or two. The money saved and the availability of food animals is worth the effort.

BREEDING SCORPIONS

Nearly all scorpion births in captivity are from females that have been inseminated in the wild before being captured. Very few have been captive bred.

Captive Breeding

As with any species taken from the wild, a captive-breeding project should be undertaken to produce a viable healthy supply for the future. There is an important lesson to be learned from tarantula keepers—captive breeding is a necessary part of advancing the hobby. Because Mexico has completely closed the exportation of animals, several species of indigenous tarantulas would not be available if a few visionary avocational keepers had not undertaken concerted captive-breeding programs.

Emperor Scorpions are the most likely candidates for captive breeding because they readily produce sizable, easy-to-care-for young (usually as many as 15). Some other scorpion taxa have been bred sporadically, but a great deal of natural history and reproductive information needs to be obtained to ensure consistent results. This will take some time and dedication.

Before a successful captive mating can occur, preparations must be undertaken. To

A mother African Flat-rock Scorpion (**Hadogenes troglodytes**) *dwarfs one of her second instar young.*

better understand the process, you should know some scorpion natural history.

Reproduction in nature is cyclic, controlled by interrelated environmental factors, including weather, temperature, and possibly photoperiods. The stimuli are so instinctive and complex that they may be all but impossible to duplicate in captivity. Fortunately, strides have been made in understanding how natural factors affect the reproduction of amphibians and reptiles that had evaded attempts at breeding in captivity for years. Controlling the temperature, humidity, and climatic cycles has made breeding many of these species commonplace. There is no reason to believe that "difficult-to-breed scorpions" will not react to similar husbandry methods.

Males and Females

As basic as it seems, being certain that you have an adult sexual pair is paramount. Adults have fully developed reproductive systems and are able to breed. Subadults cannot mate but may have obvious secondary sexual characteristics. Determining the sex of certain taxa is relatively simple, but with others it takes some experience and careful observation. Eventually, sexing scorpions becomes less difficult, but even advanced scorpion keepers make mistakes on some species. Sexually dimorphic characters are much simpler to see if several specimens of the same species are available for comparison. This may be best done when purchasing the animals, when there are many to select from. Unless the seller is really knowledgeable about scorpions, his selection may not be reliable. You should check for yourself.

Basic Differences

Generally, adult males are smaller and less bulky than females. This is particularly apparent in *Pandinus* and *Heterometrus* where females may be huge. In many species, the segments of a male's metasoma are more elongated than the female's, making it noticeably longer. There is a perceptible difference in the metasoma length of *Hadogenes* and many *Centruroides.*

The size, massiveness, and amount of granulation are greater on the "pincers" of males, particularly *Pandinus, Heterometrus,* and *Opistophthalmus.* Pedipalps of some male scorpions are thinner and longer than the female's, whereas in others only the pincers are elongated. These latter traits are found in *Centruroides* and *Heterometrus.* It may not be as obvious, but males of most forms have more prominent granulation over the surface of their exoskeletons. Some have prominent protrusions on their pedipalps and metasomas. However, this is not true in *Tityus* and *Centruroides.*

Sexual Characteristics

The comb-like pectines frequently offer a good, quick-to-recognize secondary sex characteristic. In most taxa, males have longer pectines that frequently curve slightly and possess a higher number of "teeth" than females. The safest way to check pectines is to place the scorpion in a shallow clear plastic container

with a paper towel or sponge applying some pressure from above. Turn the container upside down and start counting "teeth." A plastic, disposable petri dish is an excellent choice, and clear plastic sandwich bags will work. The scorpion will usually not be able to right itself for several seconds or longer. Unless there is a very obvious difference in pectines' size, check for other characters.

An almost foolproof method is to look closely at the genital operculum. It will require careful scrutiny and possibly the use of a magnifying glass to be sure. Males of most species have a pair of tiny protrusions (genital papillae) at the rear of the genital operculum. Again, this method is not foolproof, but is reliable for most species.

Of the available "pet" scorpions, *Hadrurus* is one of the more difficult to sex, because none of these characteristics are easily definable. Although dozens of additional sexually dimorphic characters are found among scorpions, they are specific to species and space does not permit addressing them here. In the normal course of becoming more involved with keeping scorpions, you will investigate the available literature and learn more about their natural history.

A "Romantic" Atmosphere

Tropical scorpions sometimes mate more than once throughout the year. For the others, mating is a seasonal activity, guided by climate and weather. In regions where there is a change of seasons, scorpions cease feeding at the advent of winter and retire to a shelter, remaining dormant until the temperature rises in the spring.

Rainfall is generally associated with spring-time and may be a stimulus for mating. In arid regions, during long, hot, dry spells, scorpions go into a dormant stage known as aestivation. Prey is much scarcer until the summer rains start. Altering these climatic conditions has been very successful in sexually arousing reptiles and amphibians. This concept is a starting point; there are many gray areas and still more unknowns when it comes to keeping scorpions in captivity.

Female scorpions should be well established in their cages, with satisfactory substrate, hiding places, and a smooth flat rock approximately twice the size of the female. Do not completely clean and refurbish the cage within a month of cooling or before attempting to breed them, as they must not undergo such stress.

Although it may not be necessary with some taxa, a cooling period of a month or two during the winter seems to be a good idea. The potential problem here is that there is a difference in seasons between the northern and southern hemispheres. Winter in the north is summer in the south and vice versa.

Also, it might be beneficial to not feed them, keep them away from light, and avoid disturbing them. Scorpions are sensitive to vibrations, and this may be more of a factor than has been realized. The drop in temperature should not be extreme, somewhere between 15 and 20°F (8.3–11°C) lower than the normal temperature. As a precaution against dehydrating, a shallow dish of water should be available.

At the selected time, bring the environment back to its usual state. Wait a few days for the scorpions to acclimate, and offer food. The females will be ravenous. The males may not feed, will likely be unsettled, and may wander about their cages. This is a sign that they are preparing to find a mate. Continue feeding as much as they will eat for a few weeks until they are fat and healthy.

To simulate rain, starting in the second week, moderately mist the cage—not the scorpions directly—once a day for a few days. Mist the cage just enough to moisten the surface and raise the humidity but not cause saturation and flooding. Take extreme care when misting the cages of desert scorpions; they may become totally stressed or actually drown if partially submerged.

Some desert scorpions may be stimulated to breed by having the temperature elevated to near 95°F (35°C) for a few weeks during the summer months and being misted a few times at the end of this period. This would coincide with the advent of their normal rainy season.

Making Certain One Will Not Be the Other's Lunch

Starting at dusk, there will be noticeable activity in communal cages, with males pursuing females and possibly sparring with other males. If they are fighting, their pincers are folded back and they will be pushing each other. When mating, the pincers are used to pull and clasp each other. With the room lights out, the entire proceedings can be observed with UV light. This may give you the opportunity to rescue the occasional male that might be killed by an overly aggressive cage mate. Smaller males are more likely to be harassed and injured by larger ones. Regardless, the scorpion mating ritual is a complex, fascinating act of nature to watch.

If living individually, the male should be placed in a small container and released into

the female's cage, as far away from her as possible. Do this as gingerly as possible to prevent agitating or stressing either animal. The following is a hypothetical but typical mating sequence. It is important to note that scorpion courtship varies greatly from family to family and species to species. I must admit that it is very difficult to report this without strong anthropocentric overtones.

In a few minutes, the male begins to explore his new surroundings and sense the female's presence. Some (perhaps all) females emit sex pheromones (volatile chemical substances) that inform the male that she is nearby and receptive. He begins juddering, rapidly moving his legs and shaking his body, sending vibrations through the substrate.

The female recognizes his presence through these vibrations and leaves her hiding place. She rushes at him in a mock attack; sometimes striking with her metasoma, the telson safely tucked under. They move apart, and a series of additional mock attacks are initiated. In some instances, the male stings an intersegmental membrane of the female's body, leaving the aculeus imbedded for as long as 20 minutes. If venom is injected, it likely anesthetizes and calms her, preventing normal aggressive, cannibalistic tendencies.

Facing each other, he grabs her pedipalps with his, and they dance about. This *promenade à deux* continues (usually lasting 5 minutes to an hour) until the male, using his pectines, finds a suitable surface on which to

The longer metasoma of the African Flat-rock Scorpion (Hadogenes troglodytes) in the upper part of the photograph shows it to be a male. The other is a female.

The longer and more numerous comb-like prominences of the pectines of the Thailand Forest Scorpion (Heterometrus spinifer) *on the left show it to be a male; the other is a female.*

place his spermatophore. In this situation, it is the flat rock. He deposits the stalked, free-standing spermatophore from his genital oper-culum and maneuvers her over it. She lowers her forebody toward him, squats, and forces the spermatophore into her operculum. Pres-sure caused by her moving backwards releases the sperm into her reproductive tract. He paci-fies her by grabbing and rubbing her chelicerae with his. The "kiss" continues for the brief, quiet period when she is taking in the sper-matophore.

Immediately the pair unclasps. The female remains over the spermatophore stalk for a few seconds, swaying back and forth. Material from the spermatophore plugs the opening of her operculum preventing other males from being able to inseminate her. The male attempts a hasty retreat to prevent becoming a meal. However, nearly a third of the time, males fail in this endeavor. Needless to say, if the male survives the mating he should be immediately removed. In the wild, some males may mate as many as a dozen times in a season, with several

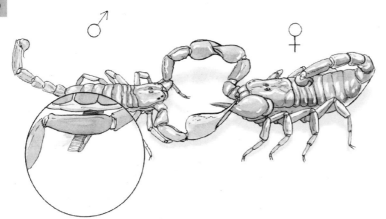

The initial contact between a pair of scorpions that are preparing to mate. The inset shows the male's extended right pectin.

females. The time needed to produce a new spermatophore is not known, but only one is present for a mating.

When a Male Is Simply Not Needed

Sperm from one mating can be retained within a female Buthid for quite some time, enabling up to four litters to be produced without remating. The number of litters from one mating is not known for other families. This explains why captive females seem to spontaneously become pregnant when there are no males present. It is fairly common for recently captured females to be pregnant or carrying sperm.

Parthenogenesis

One species of Devil Scorpion (*T. serratus*) has no males; it reproduces by parthenogenesis. Parthenogenesis is an unusual form of reproduction where offspring are produced without the need for sperm to fertilize the egg. Some Asian populations of a widely distributed scorpion, *Liocheles australasiae*, have reproduced parthenogenically. Although common in insects, it is rare in arachnids. As more research is done and additional observations are made, it seems logical that other scorpions will be found to be reproducing by this asexual method.

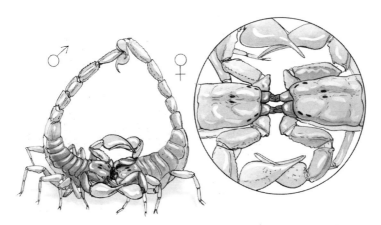

The part of the mating "dance" where the male and female are fully engaged. The inset shows the "kiss" (interlocking chelicerae), and the male grasping the female's pincers.

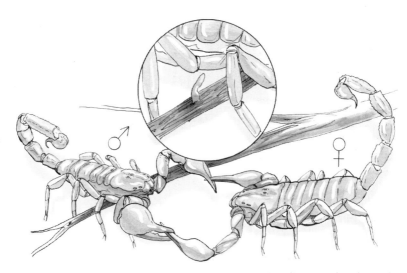

The male attempting to guide the female over the spermatophore he has attached to a twig beneath him. The inset shows the spermatophore.

Pregnancy

Gestation may take as little as two or as long as 18 months, with little visible sign of anything happening for most of that time. The female should be maintained normally. But to ensure adequate growth of the embryos, pay special attention to keeping the cage at the warmer end of its range, and be certain that the female is more than adequately fed. Underfed, pregnant females will absorb some or all of their embryos.

During the last month or so of gestation, the female's mesosoma will expand noticeably, giving the appearance of having eaten a huge meal. The intersegmental membranes will be stretched to their limit. Frequently, dozens of miniature, white scorpions will be visible within her. Eventually, she will reduce the size of meals and may refuse to feed completely. It is wise to remove pregnant females from community cages because larger scorpions will surely eat a great number of the babies when they are born.

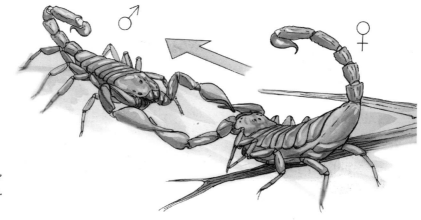

The male has pulled and positioned the female over the spermatophore.

Once again, fresh water should always be available. Her temperament will probably turn aggressive, and she will become more reclusive, possibly not venturing out of hiding at all. Do not disturb her in any way. Stress may cause her to absorb the embryos.

Birth

In a week or so, the female will surface with a few to perhaps a hundred (depending on the taxon) small, chunky, white, newborn scorpions covering her back. All scorpions give birth to living young instead of laying eggs. This may take from a few hours to a few days to complete. The size of the newborns varies from species to species. Larger scorpions tend to

A pregnant Arizona Hairy Scorpion (Hadrurus arizonensis) gave birth a week after the photograph was taken and ate all the young the next day.

have fewer and larger young, while smaller species may have a great number of tiny ones. As each newborn passes through the genital aperture, the mother helps it with her front feet. The newborns immediately climb the mother's legs onto her back where they ride for several days, until their first molt.

Stress must be kept at a minimum because mother scorpions under duress may cannibalize their young. She should be fed as much as she

A clutch of first instar Gambian Emperor Scorpions (Pandinus gambiensis) *cling to their mother's back.*

Several second instar Florida Bark Scorpions (Centruroides hentzi) *remain with their mother for a brief period before setting out for a life on their own.*

will eat to restore the nutrients used in producing the young, and she may drink a lot of water. Be certain to remove uneaten live crickets because they will eat young scorpions.

Scorpions from temperate regions usually give birth in the spring or fall, while tropical forms may do so during any season.

Raising Newborns

Newborn scorpions do not need food for a week or so, living off of stored nutrients until after their first molt. However, they are highly susceptible to desiccation and will frequently die if taken from their mother before their first molt. Scientists studying scorpion reproduction hypothesize that the time newborn scorpions spend on their mother's back is an important way of providing them with a regulated moisture gradient.

Mother's Protection of Newborns

Because newborn scorpions are almost helpless and extremely vulnerable for the first week to ten days of their lives, their mother's protection is preeminent to their survival. She may aggressively chase or kill other scorpions that get too near. Things change after the babies undergo their first molt.

A few days after molting the young begin to darken as their exoskeleton hardens. They will leave their mother periodically and begin to

Instars

Instars are the times in an arachnid's life between molts. They are sequentially numbered and the last one is when sexual maturity (adulthood) is attained.

look for food. When frightened, they scurry back to her for protection. In a few more days they will leave and begin to fend for themselves. Mother Emperor Scorpions show continued maternalism—they feed their young. By killing, crushing, and tearing open prey that is too big for the babies, she enables them to feed on the softer inner tissues. Other mother scorpions are said to demonstrate similar maternal behavior.

Things to Be Aware Of

The young of many tropical scorpions need high humidity and temperatures to feed, grow, and molt without problems. Emperor Scorpion babies thrive in moist environments, not soaking, but very damp, with near 100% humidity and temperatures of 90–100°F (32.2–37.8°C). Immature Forest Scorpions prefer similar conditions. It is a good idea to lightly mist a portion of the cages of most other scorpions with young.

Hairy Scorpions and other obligate burrowing mother scorpions are extremely cannibalistic. If stressed or if conditions are not right, she simply eats her young. It may be that birthing normally occurs within her burrow, and the babies do not leave until they have molted and are ready to fend for themselves. If you are fortunate to have them successfully go through their first molt, they should be immediately separated from their mother. Because the young are cannibalistic, they should be placed in individual containers.

For some unknown reason, very few keepers have been able to raise Hairy Scorpion young beyond the first few instars; they have trouble molting completely. It is apparent that their environmental and dietary needs are not being met. It seems to be humidity related, but it may be the type of soil they require for burrowing into or some other unknown, unexpected variable. This is one of those challenges that wait to be solved by a dedicated keeper.

Feeding the Little Guys

The biggest problem with raising newborn scorpions is providing prey small enough for them to eat. Babies of the larger taxa (*Pandinus, Heterometrus,* and *Hadogenes*) are big enough to eat small crickets and mealworms, but most of the other scorpions are too small. Some will eat freshly killed larger insects that have been crushed to expose the moist inner tissues. Unfortunately, most will require an almost constant supply of minute insects.

Pinhead crickets can be purchased at some pet shops and are a near-perfect food animal for very small scorpions. Wingless fruit flies *(Drosophila)* are an excellent, easy-to-raise food source, but they are difficult to purchase anywhere except from mail-order suppliers. The best way of having small food animals available is to raise your own fruit flies. This takes a commitment and time, because they require reculturing every 2 or 3 weeks.

One method that seems cruel to many is to allow the immature scorpions to cannibalize each other until a manageable number of the healthiest is obtained. As cruel as this first appears, it is a common happenstance in nature. Some species have dozens of babies, many of which may not be strong or healthy enough to survive anyway. Also, it permits keepers to devote their energy and resources on raising the healthiest animals available. Regardless of the amount of care given to rearing young, it is inevitable that most will not grow to adulthood. As few as 1% survive to adulthood in the wild.

It may be redundant, but maintaining proper humidity is a serious consideration when trying to raise immature scorpions. Many taxa are prone to desiccate very rapidly, and some moisture appears to aid molting. A very shallow dish of water should be provided at all times. Gravel or a small piece of sponge or gravel must be placed in the dish so that the scorpions can escape and not drown. Extreme care must be taken with very small species. Capillary action from the water surface can hold them, covering their spiracles and drowning them.

SCORPION HEALTH

Normal Development

There are several considerations that influence a scorpion's normal development and subsequent maturity. The key here is normal development. To keep them successfully, it is necessary to provide the parts of their natural history that are most important to them. As we have seen, they actually require very little attention compared with most animals.

Scorpions will grow faster if they are fed frequently and kept at higher temperatures. However, rapid growth is not necessarily a valued asset. Normal development of all the organs of their bodies so that they are capable of functioning appropriately is the primary consideration. Seasonal changes in climate and temperature are sound husbandry practices.

A Cooling Period

As discussed earlier in the chapter on breeding, a 1- or 2-month cooling period has been suggested to initiate reproduction, as was a slight drop in evening temperatures to help adjust the daily cycle. These may also act as rest times for the body. It appears to be merited to coordinating environmental changes with a regulated feeding regimen that includes periods of heavy feeding and others of deprivation.

A healthy scorpion, like this Striped-tailed Scorpion (Vaejovis spinigerus), is alert and aware of its surroundings.

Stress

As we have seen, scorpions have excellent sensing abilities and are extremely susceptible to outside influences. To use human terms, they are nervous and high-strung. Behavioral biologists call it stress. However, unlike humans where stress is complicated with psychological factors (e.g., emotions), stress in arachnids is a completely innate basic physical reaction to physical stimuli. Scorpions are very simple forms of life maintaining a highly preconditioned lifestyle. Almost anything out of the ordinary will induce some form of stress. It may cause abnormal behavioral patterns that are detrimental to the health of the scorpion. The keeper must be constantly aware to avoid situations that will stress their scorpions.

The most obvious reaction to stress is the defensive posture assumed when confronted. The immediate reactions to being uncovered or exposed to light—digging, fleeing, and defensive positioning—are additional easily noticeable negative responses. Some remain motionless or turn slowly, as if to say, "Hey, who turned on the lights?" Other scorpions react by refusing to feed, while others become aggressive to cage mates, to the point of turning to cannibalism. This is mostly apparent in stressed mother scorpions that suddenly cannibalize their young.

Light Cycles and Vibrations

Two subjects that are rarely considered or discussed are the consequences of day–night light cycles and ambient vibrations. Both are very important to a scorpion's daily survival, but what about the relationship to seasonal changes and stress?

Light cycles: We know that a scorpion's eyes function little more than to see light and dark and to inform them that it is time to begin nocturnal activities. Some arachnologists suggest that they can see stars and employ celestial navigation to move about. Research has shown that many lower and higher forms of animal life have varying degrees of this ability. Also, there is the relationship between seeing and the daily physical and behavioral activities that are inborn, being mostly controlled by the body's circadian rhythm. When taken on the seasonal level, it appears that their eyes must have some relationship and implication with reproduction.

Vibrations: Vibrations offer a completely different view on keeping scorpions in captivity. It is obvious that air and ground vibrations are extremely important to the scorpion's daily activities. Not the least of these is the stress caused by the reaction to unfamiliar, abnormal vibrations.

Humans interpret music as stimulating, soothing, exciting, etc., and we can control the quality and loudness to our preferences. Music and voices from radios and televisions reverberate throughout our homes almost constantly. No doubt, a scorpion's sensors pick up these sounds. After all, music is nothing more than a wide variety of vibrations. How does music affect scorpions? It surely cannot be soothing!

What about footsteps and the plethora of other sounds that we produce but manage to "tune out"? Practically none of the vibrations of the human's world are commonly encountered in nature. Sit quietly, and absorb the daily sounds that constantly inundate our senses. When you isolate and focus on the variety of sounds, you will find them incredibly stressful. Think of the possible effect it has on scorpions.

Subtle Annoyances

Many reactions are subtle, so much so that they may be overlooked. Usually they are related to environmental circumstances. Scorpions that climb and sit atop cage furnishings may indicate that the substrate is too wet. Spending an inordinate amount of time in the water dish may mean it is too dry. Prowling the cage, particularly during daylight hours, is a signal that something is not right.

It may be as simple as the scorpion being hungry; however the scorpion may be uncomfortable in its surroundings. This could be caused by a variety of things: too wet or dry, too hot or cold, wrong or dirty substrate, inadequate hiding places, or need for a place to molt. The movement of uneaten and unwanted live prey can be a tactile or sensory annoyance, or (a worst-case scenario) the scorpion may be infested with mites.

Parasites

Mites

Mites are diminutive, almost microscopic parasites that attach themselves to the intersegmental membranes and feed on the scorpion's tissues. They are nocturnal and seen as tan or white specks on the scorpion. If the infestation is seriously out of control, hundreds may be found slowly crawling on the cage walls or drowned in the water dish. A magnifying glass discloses their eight legs, making identification positive. They are arachnids and belong to a large diverse order acarina (20,000 described species) that includes ticks. There are several varieties of mites that affect scorpions, and they may be host-specific. Under normal conditions, scorpions tolerate a few mites, but heavy infestations can be bothersome.

Mites can be mechanically removed with small forceps or suffocated with a very small drop of glycerin or fingernail polish. Great care must be taken to avoid getting the substance in the scorpion's chelicerae and spiracles. Thoroughly wash the entire cage with diluted chlorine bleach (a 10% solution is perfect), and completely rinse it with copious amounts of water to remove any chemical residue.

Replace the substrate and cage furnishings. The furnishings can be soaked in the chlorine solution, but must be washed completely afterward. Soaps, liquid cleaners (including window cleaners), and disinfectants should not be used because they may leave harmful residues. In the wild, subadults shed mites when they molt, leaving them with the discarded exoskeleton.

Mites enter a collection by being carried on food animals, particularly crickets and roaches. They reproduce in moist substrate, not on the scorpions. The eggs hatch, find a host (e.g., scorpion), feed, drop off, and breed, continuing the cycle. Eventually, hundreds of thousands of mites may be produced, and, if left unchecked, will probably infest your entire scorpion collection. Warm, damp cages with dead and decaying cricket carcasses are the ultimate breeding grounds. Good housekeeping is an excellent preventative method.

The eggs of some mites are found in dry grains and grain products. However, aside from their unsightly infestations, they seem to do no harm to scorpions. Microwaving all grains before using them as food for prey animals and keeping them fairly dry will prevent the possibility of an epidemic.

Predatory mites: Keepers with large collections of arachnids use a biological control to eliminate parasitic mites. Predatory mites *(Hypoaspis miles)* are released into infectious cages and seek out and eat the parasitic mites. A few scientific supply companies and arachnid dealers, mostly those dealing in tarantulas, are the best sources. They are used in agriculture to control Spider Mites on plants. These mites do not seem to bother scorpions or tarantulas, but do a great job of exterminating their vexatious relatives.

Internal Parasites

Wild-caught scorpions carry a variety of internal parasites. These normally cause no harm until the animal undergoes severe stress. As has been seen in other animals brought into captivity, particularly amphibians and reptiles, internal parasites can be a serious, debilitating health hazard. Because so little is known about scorpion parasitology and nothing is known about medical treatment, death is commonly inevitable when the delicate balance is upset. The best preventative is to avoid stressing them.

Internal parasites are mostly acquired from wild food animals and are not often passed on from mothers to offspring. Hopefully, nearly every desirable scorpion species will be available from captive breeding, so many natural parasites will be lost in these captive animals. This has proved to be the case in many different

The molts of several different scorpions show that they retain some darker pigment.

kinds of animals that have been established and bred in captivity for several generations.

Growth and Molting

As a scorpion grows, its hard exoskeleton becomes too small to contain the growing internal structures, so the body forms a new larger one to replace it. The process seems simple enough, but is extremely complex.

Basically, a new outer exoskeleton forms beneath the current one. When it has developed sufficiently, the scorpion goes into hiding, some remaining motionless for as long as a day. Blood pressure is increased, causing the old exoskeleton to crack along the side and at the front of the prosoma. During the next half day, the appendages are pulled from the old skin in a series of rapid movements followed by periods of rest. All external parts, including the setae, are replaced by a molt. The shed is a translucent replica of the scorpion and retains the ability to fluoresce.

The newly molted emergent scorpion is white and extremely soft bodied. Needless to say, it is extremely vulnerable at this time. It is interesting that they do not fluoresce in this state. As the new exoskeleton darkens and hardens, the ability to fluoresce returns. The fluorescent material is only found in one layer of the "cured" exoskeleton.

Other than size, no structures are added or deleted during all the molts except the first and last ones. Actually, that is not totally true; appendages that have been broken off might partially regenerate. Little has been reported about the extent of regeneration in scorpions, but total regeneration of parts is common in some other arachnids, particularly spiders.

Changes at the First Molt

Important physical changes occur with the first molt. This includes formation of most setae, surface granulation, teeth on the cutting edges of the pincers and chelicerae, and hardening of the chelicerae, pincers, and telson. Secondary sex characters are prominently differentiated in the adult (last) molt. Although no one is certain if scorpions molt after they have reached adulthood, several researchers have reported that males, at least, do not. Wild-caught adult scorpions have worn chelae and tarsal structures that support the hypothesis that they do not molt after maturing. It seems the females of long-lived taxa would have to. Because they may live 15 years or longer beyond the adult molt, the daily physical abuse and abrasion to the exoskeleton

The same molts fluoresce in slightly different hues under a black light.

would wear it thin over time. Yet another idea to be investigated.

Scorpions molt an average of six times before reaching maturity, with five to nine reported as the extremes. It may take from 6 months to more than 7 years for a scorpion to attain adulthood. Again, it varies among different taxa. Smaller species mature rapidly, reproduce earlier, gestate for briefer periods, and have shorter life spans. Larger taxa (e.g., *Pandinus*, *Heterometrus*, and *Hadogenes*) are at the other end of the scale.

Preventing Injuries

Communally kept scorpions periodically undergo territorial skirmishes and fights. Sometimes it gets a bit rough, and an appendage may be damaged or torn off. Of course, there is always the possibility of fatal envenomation or cannibalism. The latter can be a serious problem for a scorpion that has just molted. During the week to 10 days it takes for the exoskeleton to harden following a molt, the scorpion is very susceptible to predation or injury by a cage mate. These are the chances taken in communal situations. Having a cage large enough to adequately accommodate the animals, providing plenty of hiding places, and being certain they are well fed will help prevent difficulties.

Cage furnishings used as retreats should be placed or stacked in a way that they will not fall and crush the captive. This is particularly important with scorpions that dig a lot. Curls of cork bark make excellent lightweight retreats. Remember that scorpions like to be in contact with the walls of their tunnels or scrapes. Adding a cactus to a desert cage gives it esthetic appeal, but increases the chance of an injury. Many cacti and succulents have extremely sharp spines that could pierce the softer parts of a scorpion's body. I suggest you use plastic substitutes if you think you must decorate your cages.

Even though the exoskeleton is hard, it is not a foolproof protection. It is highly susceptible to cracking if impacted. Potentially, the most menacing cause of this type of injury is a fall. It is unlikely that it will happen in a cage, since the height is rarely enough to permit a serious fall. Damaging falls usually occur during transporting, cage cleaning, and handling.

Whenever a scorpion is taken from its cage, it should be enclosed in a covered container. There are few things more tragic and frustrating for a keeper than watching a scorpion lying on the floor, motionless, as body fluids ooze from a split in its mesosomal membrane. In all but a very few cases, there is nothing that can be done to close the wound and save the animal. It is best destroyed to stop its suffering.

Applying something to cover, clot, or gel leaking hemolymph may close a small wound, but a large one will probably cause the scorpion to "bleed" to death. In the wild, many small injuries are sealed when particles of sand or soil adhere to the hemolymph, effectively closing the wound. In captivity, talcum powder or a dab of nail polish have been effective in some instances. A variety of products known as "liquid skin," sold in pharmacies for closing small cuts to human skin, also work. Taking great care to avoid an accident is the only proven cure.

Proper Humidity

Water is a necessary part of all living cells and must be renewed periodically. Scorpions are known to drink water, but most of it is taken from the food they eat. Aside from these sources, at the very least, some moisture appears to be necessary for scorpions to survive.

Scorpions from tropical rainforests rely heavily on external sources, whereas those from extremely arid areas may accept it opportunistically. First instars will desiccate if they are deprived of moisture provided from contact with their mother. It is conjectured that scorpions cannot absorb moisture from their environment through their hardened exoskeletons. This may or may not be true. Some water may be passed through the intersegmental membranes. Water is lost through the unhardened skin of

newly molted scorpions, and it is highly likely that absorption is possible at that time as well.

Desert species frequently live in burrows or under rocks and ground debris—places that maintain some moisture. Scorpion burrows are reported to retain relative humidity as high as 50–70%. This may provide cooling by evaporation and may be important to the molting process. Numerous species remain dormant during the driest months, coming to the surface with the advent of summer rains. In many desert regions, morning dew forms on rocks, plants, and other objects (including the exposed bodies of some animals), and it is regularly drunk by lizards, insects, and other small animals. There is no reason that scorpions would not do likewise.

One way to partially avoid the potential desiccation problem is to provide a shallow dish of water for all scorpions. Those requiring high humidity (e.g., tropical rainforest scorpions) should have water at all times, and their cages should be lightly misted every few days. The substrate should never be allowed to dry out completely.

Scorpions from unknown microhabitats should have water available and should be tested (as suggested in the section on cage furnishings) to determine their needs. Subadult and small forms from all but the most arid environments can desiccate rapidly, so their water supplies should be monitored often. Because more scorpions die from desiccation than starvation, it behooves the keeper to make fresh water available.

GLOSSARY

The following words have been taken in their relationship with scorpions; they may have additional meanings in different contexts.

Aculeus: the sharp, pointed barb on the telson through which venom is injected.

Aestivation: a state of dormancy similar to hibernation, but initiated by heat and dry conditions.

Arthropod: the largest invertebrate phylum (more than 800,000 species) with segmented bodies, jointed appendages, and chitinous exoskeleton.

Basitarus: the terminal section of a scorpion's leg.

Book lungs: respiratory organs that exchange gasses between the outside and hemolymph.

Bristlecombs: clumps of setae that (on the feet) better enable walking on sand or (in the preoral cavity) strain indigestible food particles.

Carapace: dorsal plate at the fore-portion of the prosoma; contains eyes and partially covers chelicerae.

Chelae: the pair of pincerlike ("hand") sections of the pedipalps; each is comprised of a movable "finger" and a stationary manus ("palm"). (chela = singular form)

Circadian rhythm: physiologic or behavioral changes in synch with a 24-hour cycle apparently only partially related to the day and night cycle.

Chitin: the hard, partially flexible, insoluble, organic substance that gives stability and physical integrity to the exoskeleton.

C.I.T.E.S. (Convention on the International Trade of Endangered Species): an international association of countries formed to control the exportation of endangered wildlife and plants.

Conspecifics: animals of the same species.

Exoskeleton: hard, chitinous outer skin of the scorpion; it supports the weight of the body and contains the internal organs.

Fossorial: living in the ground.

Genital operculum: external opening of the reproductive tract.

Hemolymph: clear, almost colorless fluid in arthropods that functions as blood.

Intersegmental membrane: the flexible membrane connecting the segments of the exoskeleton and that allows movement.

Lithophile: living among rocks.

Littoral: living within a tidal zone.

Mesosoma: the large, segmented portion of the body between the prosoma and metasoma.

Obligate burrower: digs its own burrow.

Pheromone: a volatile chemical secreted by a member of a taxon as a signal to (mostly) other members of that taxon.

Psammophile: living in sand.

Scrape: a small cavern under a stone or ground litter that has been cleared and enlarged by a scorpion.

Sexual dimorphism: physical characters that differentiate males from females.

Spermatophore: an adhering mass (package) of sperm and fluids deposited by the male to be picked up by the female to fertilize her eggs.

Sternite: one of the five ventral segments of the mesosoma.

Tarsus: a scorpion's "foot."

Terrestrial: living on or in the surface litter of the ground.

Trichobothria: long, thin setae ("hair") that are incredibly sensitive to air movements and vibrations. They are found only on a scorpion's pedipalps and are important identification characters.

Troglobite: living in caves with no light or the barest amount.

Troglophile: living in the entrances to caves.

Vesicle: the rounded, bulbous part of the telson in which venom is stored.

Arthropod Societies

These organizations publish journals, newsletters, and/or arachnid-related materials, and membership is highly recommended to serious scorpion enthusiasts. Dues are required.

American Tarantula Society
P.O. Box 1617
Artesia, NM 88211

American Arachnological Society
c/o Dr. Norman Platnick
AMNH
Central Park West at 79th Street
New York, NY 10024

British Arachnological Society
c/o S. H. Hexter
71 Havant Road
Walthamstow, London E17 3JE England

British Tarantula Society
c/o Ann Webb
81 Phillimore Place
Radlett, Hertfordshire WD7 8NJ England

Young Entomologist's Society
1915 Peggy Place
Lansing, MI 48910-2553

Suggested Reading

The following publications are excellent sources of information about scorpions and are in print or available at major libraries.

Brodie, E. D. *Venomous Animals. (A Golden Guide).* New York, NY: Golden Press, 1989.

Brownell, P. H., and G. A. Polis, eds. *Scorpion Biology and Research.* Oxford, England: Oxford University Press, 1999.

Dunn, G. A. *Caring for Insect Livestock: An Insect Rearing Manual.* Special Pub. #8. Lansing, MI: Young Entomologist's Society, 1993.

_____. *The Insect Study Source Book: An International Entomology Resource Guide* (5th Ed.). Special Pub. #1. Lansing, MI: Young Entomologist's Society, 1995.

Fet, V., W. D. Sissom, G. Lowe, and M. Braunwalder. *Catalog of the Scorpions of the World (1758–1997).* New York, NY: New York Entomological Society, 1999.

Gaban, R. D. *Gaban's Scorpion Tales.* Artesia, NM: American Tarantula Society, 1998.

Jackman, J. A. *A Field Guide to the Spiders and Scorpions of Texas.* Houston, TX: Texas Monthly Press, 1997.

Keegan, H. L. *Scorpions of Medical Importance.* Jackson, MS: University of Mississippi, 1980.

Levi, H. W., and L. R. Levi. *Spiders and Their Kin (A Golden Guide).* New York, NY: Golden Press, 1990.

Marshall, S. D. *Tarantulas and Other Arachnids.* Hauppauge, NY: Barron's Educational Series, Inc., 1996.

Polis, G., ed. *Biology of Scorpions.* Palo Alto, CA: Stanford University Press, 1990.

Pringle, L. *Scorpion Man: Exploring the World of Scorpions.* New York, NY: Charles Scribner's Sons, 1994.

Arachnological Publication Sources

Paul Gritis Books
P.O. Box 4298
Bethlehem, PA 18018
610-954-0466

Young Entomologist's Society
1915 Peggy Place
Lansing, MI 48910-2553

Zoo Book Sales
P.O. Box 405
Lanesboro, MN 55949-0405
507-467-8735

Sources

These are some reliable sources for products that are mentioned in the text.

UV lights

Bass Pro Shops
2500 E. Kearney St.
Springfield, MO 65898

BioQuip
17803 LaSalle Avenue
Gardena, CA 90248

Crickets, mealworms, fruit flies, and other food animals and supplies

Cockroaches
Frank Holder
399 Freedom Rd.
Pleasant Valley, NY 12569
914-635-8471

Flightless House Flies
Mary Testa
P.O. Box 250
Yola, CA 95697
530-666-0321

Ghann's Cricket Farm
P.O. Box 211840
Augusta, GA 30917
800-476-2248

Grubco
Box 15001
Hamilton, OH 45015
800-222-3563

Powers Science Materials
3875 Franklin Rd.
Jackson, MS 49203
517-764-5929

Rainbow Mealworms and Crickets
126 E. Spruce St.
Compton, CA 90220
800-777-9676

Internet Sites

Logging on to any of the following stable Web sites will link you to a myriad of other related sites.

American Tarantula Society	//torgo.cnhost.com/ats
Arachnodata Home Page	//www.arachnodata.ch/welcome.htm
Arachnology Home Page	//www.dns.ufsia.be/arachnology/arachnology.html
Emperor Scorpion Home Page	//www.slip.ne/~drrod/
Scorpion Enthusiasts Forum	//wrbu.si.edu/www/stockwell/
Gordon's Entomological Home Page	//www.insect-world.com/main/scorpionidae.html
Hadrurus Page	//www.fortunecity.com/tinpan/morrissey/432/hadrurus
Singapore Scorpion Page	//sunflower.singnet.com.sg/~caijw/welcome.html
Young Entomologist's Society Home Page	//YESbugs@aol.com

Important Note

Scorpion venom is potentially dangerous, and some may be life threatening. Stings should never be taken lightly, particularly if the animal is known to have a highly toxic venom, or the keeper has been previously stung or is prone to allergic reactions.

The author and publisher recommend that scorpions should not be handled at any time. Anyone keeping scorpions must understand the potential danger to themselves and others, and take extreme measures to prevent a sting or an animal's escape. Check your state regulations to assure that you can legally keep scorpions, and to see if a permit is required.

Acknowledgments

I would like to offer special thanks to Kari McWest, David Schleser, Fred Sherberger, and David Sisson for reviewing the manuscript and offering their much-needed comments and suggestions on its content. Also, thanks to Jonathan Leeming (South Africa), Rolando Teruel Ochoa (Cuba), and Jan Ove Rein (Norway) for their input and help with the captive condition tables. I would be remiss if I did not mention the dozens of scorpion cyber buddies, worldwide, who unselfishly pass along their observations and findings with the hope of furthering the hobby of scorpion keeping.

Final Thoughts

If you go into the field and collect scorpions, please take the utmost care to replace objects you turn and always be aware that you are impacting the environment. Every attempt should be made to leave everything as close as possible to how you found it. Take only the animals that you can properly care for.

It takes very little time and energy for you to make a contribution to the science of arachnology. By keeping accurate notes of exactly where animals were captured and the conditions at the site, the animal has continuing value even when it has died. Preserving scorpions is easy. Simply submerse the dead animal in a small container of rubbing (isopropyl) alcohol and include a label with its collecting data. It is imperative that the information is accurate.

Contact a local natural history museum or college biology department and tell them what you have. Known as voucher specimens, these preserved animals provide an accurate identification and locality for someone studying the local scorpion fauna. It is possible that the animal has not been reported from the area, and—who knows?—it might be an undescribed species. A great deal of information has been furnished by careful, dedicated amateur arachnologists.

There is an important lesson to be learned from the hobby of herpetoculture—"Pushing" amphibians and reptiles to reach adulthood and reproduce causes many of the problems associated with their captive breeding. Arachnoculturists must not fall into this trap. As keepers, we should help their natural progression by supporting the animal's needs, rather than dictate and change them for our own whims or gain.

About the Author

Manny Rubio is a commercial photographer, author, and naturalist who has photographed wildlife throughout the world. His photographs have been widely published, and he has more than 500 magazine covers to his credit. He has written more than 100 articles, mostly on herpetology and arachnids. In 1999, Smithsonian Press published his highly acclaimed book on rattlesnakes.

Photo Credits

All photos, including covers, by Manny Rubio

All inquiries should be addressed to:
Barron's Educational Series, Inc.
250 Wireless Boulevard
Hauppauge, NY 11788
http://www.barronseduc.com

International Standard Book No. 0-7641-1224-4

Library of Congress Catalog Card No. 99-31708

Library of Congress Cataloging-in-Publication Data
Rubio, Manny.
    Scorpions : a complete pet owner's manual / Manny Rubio.
        p. cm.
        Includes bibliographical references.
        ISBN 0-7641-1224-4
        1. Scorpions as pets. I. Title.
    SF459.S35R83   2000
    639'.7—dc21   99-31708
                                                   CIP

Printed in Hong Kong

9 8 7 6 5 4 3 2 1